recipes for
weight
loss

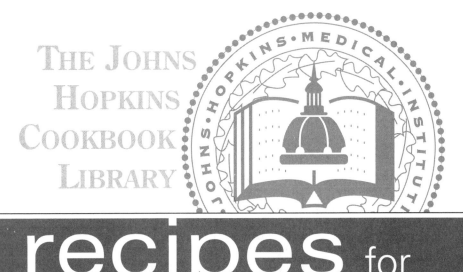

THE JOHNS
HOPKINS
COOKBOOK
LIBRARY

recipes for

weight
loss

Medical Editor

LAWRENCE J. CHESKIN, M.D.

Nutrition Editor

LORA BROWN WILDER, Sc.D., M.S., R.D.

REBUS
NEW YORK

JOHNS HOPKINS HEALTH AFTER 50 PUBLICATIONS

The Johns Hopkins Cookbook Library: Recipes for Weight Loss is one of many indispensable medical publications for consumers from America's leading health center. We publish other comprehensive reference books, including consumer guides to drugs and medical tests; White Papers that provide in-depth reports on specific disorders such as coronary heart disease, arthritis, and diabetes; and *The Johns Hopkins Medical Letter: HEALTH AFTER 50,* our monthly 8-page newsletter that presents recommendations from Hopkins experts on current medical issues that affect you.

All of our publications provide timely information—in clear, non-technical language—for everyone concerned with taking control of his or her own health. And, they all come from the century-old tradition of Johns Hopkins excellence.

For a trial subscription to our newsletter, you can call 904-446-4675 or write to Subscription Dept., Health After 50, P.O.Box 420179, Palm Coast, FL 32142.

For information on our publications—along with health and medical updates from our experts—visit our website:

www.hopkinsafter50.com

REBUS

Library of Congress Cataloging-in-Publication Data

Recipes for weight loss / medical editor, Lawrence Cheskin ; nutrition editor, Lora Brown Wilder.
    p. cm. – (The Johns Hopkins cookbook library)
   Includes index.
   ISBN 0-929661-78-8
    1. Reducing diets–Recipes. I. Cheskin, Lawrence J. II. Wilder, Lora Brown. III. Series.

RM222.2 .R426 2003
641.5'635–dc21

2002036862

Printed in the United States of America
10 9 8 7 6 5 4 3 2 1

contents

Eating for Weight Loss 6

What to Eat and Why (chart) 8

Add These Foods to Your Diet 10

The Recipes

A User's Guide 14

Appetizers & Soups 16

Fish, Meat & Poultry 31

Meatless 81

Side Dishes 100

Desserts 123

Breads & Breakfast 137

The Savvy Shopper 146

Leading Sources (nutrient charts) 152

Index 154

eating for weight loss

Along with regular exercise and not smoking, keeping your weight under control is one of the most important ways to maintain good health. Slow, gradual weight loss is healthier, easier to achieve, and more likely to be permanent than rapid weight loss. People often tend to adopt unrealistic goals and try to lose weight too quickly, which can set up a cycle of failure and discouragement. Any weight loss strategy should include foods that you will enjoy eating for the rest of your life, not just tolerate for a few weeks or months. The recipes in this book use nutritious, readily available foods that offer a wealth of sensory pleasures and satisfying flavors and textures.

Obesity has reached epidemic proportions in the United States; and excess body fat is linked to coronary heart disease, type 2 diabetes, high blood pressure, increased levels of triglycerides, low levels of HDL cholesterol, and certain types of cancer. Losing weight can decrease the risk for these conditions while enhancing energy levels and building feelings of confidence and self-esteem. Shedding even a few pounds can significantly improve general health. For example, if you are overweight, reducing your body weight by as little as 5% can lower elevated blood pressure, improve your lipid profile, and reduce the risk of developing diabetes. It can also improve or even eliminate the symptoms of sleep apnea and decrease the risk of progressive osteoarthritis in weight-bearing joints.

The secret to successful weight management is sticking to a lifelong healthy eating style (not "dieting") and getting regular exercise: You must be motivated enough to change habits not for a few weeks or months, but for a lifetime. Anyone who is over age 40 or has health problems should have a thorough medical evaluation prior to beginning a weight loss program. In addition, consult your physician or nutritionist to assess your eating habits and determine the best course of action to achieve and maintain weight loss.

cut calories

We need to take in a certain number of calories to supply the energy required for metabolism and everyday activities. If we take in more calories than are required, they are stored by the body, as fat. Therefore, weight is ultimately determined by the balance between calories consumed and calories used. And it makes no difference where these calories come from. Extra calories—whether they come from fat, carbohydrates, or proteins—contribute to weight gain. In fact, eating excessive calories than are expended along with physical inactivity are two major causes of the rising rate of obesity in the United States.

RECENT RESEARCH

PORTION DISTORTION

A new study suggests that super-size portions of food have become common in American restaurants, and the trend contributes to the increasing prevalence of overweight and obesity in the U.S.

Researchers sampled foods and beverages typically available in take-out, fast-food, and family-style restaurants. Portions were compared with original sizes available in the past and to standard serving sizes currently outlined by government agencies (USDA and FDA). Serving size information was obtained from manufacturers and from direct weighing.

The portions of almost all of the beverages and foods sampled were found to be excessive in size and significantly bigger than in the past. Cookies were found to be seven times larger than the government reference serving size, and cooked pasta, muffins, steaks, and bagels surpassed USDA serving sizes by 480%, 333%, 224%, and 195% respectively.

The researchers conclude that typical portions in family-style restaurants are oversized and portion control should be emphasized as a strategy for weight management.

AMERICAN JOURNAL OF PUBLIC HEALTH
VOLUME 92, PAGE 246
FEBRUARY 2002

reduce fat

Fat is a concentrated source of calories—9 calories per gram, compared with 4 calories per gram in protein and carbohydrates—and small amounts of fatty foods can pack a lot of calories. Simply reducing fat intake, however, does not guarantee weight loss. Overeating even low-fat foods can result in weight gain if the low-fat foods are high in calories (which they often are) or if you eat enough of them.

In addition to limiting fat for weight control, certain fats, particularly saturated fat, are harmful to your health. Foods high in saturated fat include full-fat dairy products (like cheese, whole milk, cream, butter, and regular ice cream), lard, meats (both fresh and processed), the skin and fat of poultry, as well as the palm and coconut oils used in many prepared foods. These foods can elevate harmful LDL cholesterol levels while adding extra inches to your waist. Also damaging to your health are the trans fatty acids found in packaged foods such as cookies, crackers, and other baked goods; commercially prepared fried foods; and most margarines. Look for the words "hydrogenated" or "partially hydrogenated" on the ingredient list to determine if a food contains trans fatty acids.

increase complex carbohydrates

Eating a diet rich in complex carbohydrates helps with weight loss in several ways: Complex carbohydrates can provide a satisfying volume of food with a minimum of calories, especially when they replace fat in the diet; they provide a feeling of fullness, which helps curb appetite; and many are rich in fiber, which has multiple health benefits (see below). The United States Department of Agriculture (USDA) recommends that Americans eat six to eleven servings of complex carbohydrates per day. The base of the USDA Food Guide Pyramid depicts that the bulk of what we should eat is from the complex carbohydrate group. One slice of bread, 1 ounce of ready-to-eat cereal, or ½ cup of cooked cereal, rice or pasta each constitute one serving.

get more fiber

Eating plenty of fiber-rich foods can help to maintain a proper weight. The two main types of dietary fiber—soluble and insoluble—contribute to weight control in specific ways. Soluble fiber (also called "viscous" fiber)—found in oats, barley, legumes, and dried and fresh fruit—forms a gel around food particles, which slows their passage through the stomach and delays hunger signals sent to the brain.

The other type of fiber, insoluble fiber, sometimes called "roughage," is the sponge-like form of dietary fiber found in broccoli, potatoes with their skins, apples, beans, and whole-grain breads and cereals. This type of fiber absorbs

eating for weight loss

WHAT TO EAT AND WHY		
nutrient	food sources	health benefits
complex carbohydrates	Legumes (peas, beans), starchy vegetables (such as potatoes, winter squash, corn, sweet potatoes), whole grains, and pasta	Foods rich in complex carbohydrates provide a feeling of fullness that helps to restrain appetite. Complex carbohydrate-rich foods usually provide ample amounts of vitamins, minerals, and fiber.
fiber	apples, barley, beans, broccoli, grapefruit, legumes, mushrooms, oats, pears, potatoes with their skins, dried fruit, whole-grain breads and cereals	People who eat fiber-rich diets get less hungry between meals, feel fuller more quickly at mealtime, and tend to consume fewer calories throughout the day.

water in the digestive tract, thus supplying bulk that contributes to a feeling of fullness, which helps to discourage overeating.

In addition to helping with weight loss, soluble fiber can also lower LDL cholesterol levels; insoluble fiber is useful in preventing constipation. Most high-fiber foods contain some of each type of fiber. Bulk up on both soluble and insoluble fiber by consuming a variety of fruits, vegetables, and whole-grain foods.

select low-fat sources of protein

Choosing protein-rich foods that are low in saturated fat will help to reduce your fat and calorie intake. Good low-fat sources of protein include fish, shellfish, poultry without the skin, lean cuts of meat, egg whites, and low-fat dairy foods. Good plant sources of protein include tofu and dried beans, especially soybeans. Though both tofu and soybeans can have quite a bit of fat (and calories), they are extremely low in saturated fat. In fact, most of their fat is unsaturated and includes healthful essential fatty acids such as linoleic acid and small amounts of omega-3 fatty acids. And reduced-fat tofu is now available.

increase fruits and vegetables

Unprocessed foods such as fruits and vegetables play an important role in weight loss because they are filling, and thus help to satisfy cravings, provide fiber, and can be consumed liberally if they don't have fat or sugar added to them. Rich in vitamins and minerals, most fruits and vegetables are naturally low in fat and calories, are chock full of essential nutrients, and may also supply disease-fighting antioxidants and phytochemicals. The Dietary Guidelines for Americans recommends 2 to 4 servings of fruit (e.g., 1 fruit, or ¾ cup juice) and 3 to 5 servings of vegetables (e.g., ½ cup chopped vegetables, or ½ cup tomato sauce) daily.

calorie needs for weight loss

Since everyone's dietary needs are different, be sure to consult your physician to accommodate your specific health concerns before you begin a weight loss plan. Most important, be patient and lose weight slowly: Weight loss of one to two pounds per week is considered a gradual and safe rate. And the calorie cutback need not be so severe if you also begin to exercise regularly.

To maintain weight: It takes roughly 15 calories per pound of body weight for a moderately active person (someone who gets at least 30 minutes of moderate to intense physical activity every day) to maintain weight. For example, the average moderately active 150-pound person who consumes 2,250 calories per day will neither gain nor lose weight. A completely sedentary person may require just 12 calories per pound to maintain weight.

To lose weight: A pound of body fat contains 3,500 calories. To lose one to two pounds per week you daily intake must be 500 to 1,000 calories less than what's needed to maintain your current weight. Calorie intake should not drop below 1,200 per day in women or 1,500 per day in men (unless the diet is medically supervised and you are taking a vitamin/mineral supplement), since it is difficult to get all the nutrients you need on a severely calorie-restricted diet.

the importance of exercise

While exercise alone does not lead to significant weight loss, the combination of exercise and diet leads to greater loss of weight and body fat than dieting alone, and is also associated with a greater likelihood of maintaining the weight loss. Furthermore, exercise may help you stay on a diet because it makes the cutback in calories less drastic. For example, if you engage in moderate to vigorous physical activity for 30 minutes a day you will burn about 250 calories. Because this additional calorie expenditure increases your dairy calorie needs, you can consume more calories and still lose weight, making it easier to stay on your eating plan.

Be sure, however, that you start an exercise program gradually. Sedentary people over the age of 40 should consult their doctor before starting any vigorous exercise program.

add these foods to your diet

apples

what's in it Apples provide a good amount of both insoluble and soluble fiber, including a type of soluble fiber called pectin. Studies show that soluble fiber helps to lower blood cholesterol. A number of phytochemicals found in apples are under review for potential health benefits.

cook's notes: While the soluble fiber pectin is found in both cooked and uncooked apples, cooking will help to increase its bioavailability.

beans, dried

what's in it A nourishing, low-fat source of plant protein, dried beans are high in complex carbohydrates, fiber, B vitamins (especially folate), and minerals, such as potassium, magnesium, and selenium. Beans are particularly rich in cholesterol-lowering soluble fiber. And the insoluble fiber in dried beans helps to improve regularity by speeding the passage of food through the intestine. The ample fiber content of dried beans also bolsters weight-control efforts by contributing to a feeling of fullness.

cook's notes: The gas-causing culprits in beans are carbohydrates called oligosaccharides. Some research suggests that presoaking beans, and then discarding the soaking water before cooking them, will get rid of some of the oligosaccharides.

beets

what's in it Beets are a rich source of fiber, potassium, and folate. Notable for their sweet, earthy flavor, beets have the highest sugar content of any vegetable, while remaining very low in calories (1 cup of cooked beets has only 75 calories). And unlike many other vegetables, their full flavor is retained whether they are fresh or canned (which is the way most beets are sold in the United States). Fresh beets, though, have a characteristic flavor and a crisp texture that you don't find in canned versions; and some of the B vitamins in canned beets may leach out into the packing liquid.

cook's notes: The best way to cook beets is to bake or roast them with their skins on and their stem and root ends untrimmed. The reason for this is that if you peel beets, or cut into them at all, they will leak out their deep-purple color as they cook.

broccoli

what's in it A high-fiber, nutrient-dense food, broccoli is a good source of folate, riboflavin, vitamin B_6, vitamin C, and potassium. Noted for its wealth of phytochemicals, broccoli (and especially broccoli sprouts) is a leading source of sulforaphane, a compound that helps prevent cell damage associated with aging, cancer, and other illnesses. Broccoli also contains beta carotene and lutein, carotenoids with antioxidant properties.

cook's notes: To preserve broccoli's nutrients, cook it as briefly as possible: steam, microwave, or stir-fry it. Raw broccoli has more vitamin C than cooked; however, cooking will make the carotenoids in the vegetable more bioavailable.

brussels sprouts

what's in it Along with their savory flavor and satisfying texture, Brussels sprouts offer vitamin C, fiber, folate, and other B vitamins, as well as the carotenoids lutein and zeaxanthin. In addition, because they are cruciferous vegetables, Brussels sprouts contain phytochemicals called indoles, which are thought to have cancer-fighting potential.

cook's notes: The best way to cook Brussels sprouts is to steam them, since boiling them would leach out some of their water-soluble B vitamins. If you serve Brussels sprouts with a little bit of unsaturated oil, it improves the absorption of their carotenoids, which are fat-soluble.

cabbage

what's in it Along with its distinctive flavor, cabbage has good amounts of vitamin C, folate, and fiber (1 cup of cooked cabbage provides 6.6 g and uncooked, 7.6 g of fiber), making it a nutritious food. It also contains natural plant chemicals (phytochemicals) called indoles that appear to lower the risk of hormone-related cancers.

cook's notes: Raw cabbage can be a good source of vitamin C, however, don't slice the cabbage until you are ready to use it; slicing hastens the loss of vitamin C. When cooking cabbage, it is best to steam, microwave, or stir-fry to help retain its nutrients.

cantaloupe

what's in it Low in calories and rich in potassium, vitamin B$_6$, and vitamin C, cantaloupe is an excellent source of the antioxidant beta carotene. In fact, cantaloupes provide more beta carotene than any other melon. The body converts beta carotene into vitamin A, which is important for eye health and for promoting healthy cell growth.

cook's notes: Be sure to wash the rinds of cantaloupe (as well as other melons), since they are susceptible to bacterial contamination because they grow on the ground. To preserve their nutritional content, buy whole cantaloupes rather than pre-cut halves or cubes: Vitamin C is diminished when exposed to air.

carrots

what's in it Carrots are an exceptional source of plant pigments called carotenoids, which are so named because they were first identified in carrots. Carrots are the leading source in the American diet of the antioxidant beta carotene. Along with beta carotene, carrots also supply alpha carotene and lutein, other carotenoids that have antioxidant properties. The carrots with the deepest color contain the most carotenoids.

cook's notes: Because carotenoids are fat-soluble nutrients, cooking carrots with a little bit of fat (preferably monounsaturated fat, such as canola or olive oil) or eating them with other sources of fat, makes the beta carotene more available for absorption by the body. Cooking also makes the soluble fiber in the carrots more bioavailable.

chicken

what's in it Chicken (without the skin) supplies low-fat protein and is a rich source of vitamins and minerals. Chicken is a very good source of a number of B vitamins (riboflavin, niacin, B$_6$, and B$_{12}$) as well as the minerals iron, selenium, and zinc. Although dark-meat chicken, such as as the thigh, is higher in fat (3 to 5 times higher, depending on the bird), it also brings with it a higher concentration of minerals.

cook's notes: In addition to the fat found in chicken meat, there is also a substantial amount in the skin (about half the total fat is in the skin). So although it's all right to roast, broil, or grill chicken with the skin on to preserve moisture, the skin should be removed before eating. If the chicken is cooked in a soup, stew, stir-fry, or casserole, the skin should be removed before cooking.

corn

what's in it A highly popular food, complex carbohydrate-rich corn provides fiber, thiamin, folate, potassium, iron, and magnesium. Only yellow corn, however, contains beta carotene as well as the carotenoids lutein and zeaxanthin. These two carotenoids are associated with healthy eyes and may be helpful in preventing cataracts and age-related macular degeneration.

cook's notes: To preserve the water-soluble B vitamins (folate and thiamin) in fresh corn, it's best to steam rather than boil it. If this isn't practical (since most people cook ears by the dozen), be sure to cook for no longer than 10 minutes in rapidly boiling water to minimize nutrient loss.

dairy

what's in it Low-fat (1%) or fat-free (also called skim) milk and yogurt provide high-quality protein, calcium, B vitamins (especially vitamin B12), and minerals, without the added saturated fat, which increases harmful LDL cholesterol (1% milk has a small amount of saturated fat but much less than whole milk). For the most calcium per cup, fat-free plain yogurt is the best, at 488 mg (about 40% of the recommended daily intake). After that, in descending order, are low-fat yogurt (448 mg), fat-free milk (352 mg), and 1% milk (300 mg), all excellent sources of calcium.

grains, whole

what's in it Whole-grain foods such as whole-grain breads, brown rice, and oatmeal, are high in fiber and provide complex carbohydrates, folate, riboflavin, thiamin, niacin, iron, zinc, magnesium, selenium, and vitamin E. Studies have shown that whole-grain foods help to lower the risk of type 2 diabetes and cardiovascular disease. Whole grains retain their bran (the outer layer of the grain) and the germ (the inner part), which provide nutrients and phytochemicals. Wheat bran, the outer layer of the wheat kernel, provides fiber, B vitamins, protein, and iron. The Food Guide Pyramid recommends that adults eat 6 to 11 servings of grain foods daily; several of those servings should be whole grains. Look for products with "whole grain" or "100 percent whole wheat" at the top of the ingredient list to make sure you are buying whole-grain foods. High-fiber whole grains are heart-healthy and they are also helpful in weight loss.

add these foods to your diet

grapefruit

what's in it Along with pectin (the soluble fiber that helps to lower cholesterol levels), potassium, and various types of phytochemicals, grapefruit also supplies copious amounts of vitamin C: At only about 60 calories, one half of a medium-size grapefruit will provide 110% of the current recommended daily value of this important antioxidant vitamin. Pink and red grapefruit also contain the carotenoid beta carotene. Grapefruit juice is also highly nutritious, though it lacks the fiber present in the whole fruit.

cook's notes: Don't remove all of the pith, which is the white spongy layer between the zest and the pulp, because it contains a good amount of the fruit's fiber.

grapes

what's in it While table grapes have modest amounts of vitamins and minerals; some varieties are good sources of vitamin C, and their juiciness and natural sweetness, combined with a low calorie count, make them an ideal snack food. The skins of red and purple grapes (as well as red and purple grape juice and red wine) contain a substance called resveratrol. Animal studies indicate that resveratrol may lower LDL cholesterol and have anticlotting effects.

greens

what's in it Cooking greens— once relegated to regional or ethnic cuisines—are gaining greater recognition for their nutritional benefits. Some of the leafy greens available in the market are the tops of root vegetables (such as beet greens and turnips greens), and some are plants that are grown only for their greens, such as kale, collard greens, Swiss chard, and spinach. The most healthful greens are those with the darkest color. Many types of intensely colored leafy plants— especially kale, collards, and others in the cabbage family—are rich in beta carotene, vitamin C, folate, and other substances that may protect against cancer, heart disease, and a host of other conditions. Cooking greens are also good sources of fiber and of various minerals, particularly iron and calcium. However, although beet greens, spinach, and Swiss chard contain calcium, they also contain substances called oxalates, which prevent calcium from being properly absorbed.

cook's notes: To enhance the bioavailability of beta carotene in cooking greens, cook or eat them with a small amount of canola or olive oil. If you do cook greens in water, which can diminish folate levels, try to use the cooking water in the recipe.

lentils

what's in it An inexpensive, low-fat source of fiber, potassium, and zinc, the lentil is also a good source of B vitamins, including folate. For example, a mere ½-cup serving of lentils supplies almost half the daily requirement for this B vitamin. Plant protein and complex carbohydrates are also supplied by lentils, which have provided sustenance for humankind for thousands of years.

cook's notes: To protect the water-soluble vitamins folate and vitamin B_6, don't cook lentils in too much water; and if any cooking liquid needs to be drained off, try to use it in the recipe or save for soups or other dishes. Soluble fiber in lentils is made more bioavailable as the lentils cook and the fiber dissolves. Eat foods high in vitamin C with lentils to enhance iron absorption.

mushrooms

what's in it Mushrooms are more than just wonderful flavor enhancers: They provide riboflavin, niacin, vitamin B_6, and a type of soluble fiber called beta-glucan. And as a boon to those watching their calorie intake, mushrooms have a satisfying flavor and texture for almost no calories (2 whole cups of raw mushrooms have about 40 calories).

cook's notes: Since the B vitamins in mushrooms leach into water when heated, if you soak dried mushrooms to reconstitute them, it's best to use the soaking water in the recipe.

oil, sesame

what's in it Dark sesame oil used in cooking is pressed from roasted sesame seeds, giving the oil a deep flavor and heady fragrance. One of the side benefits of its pungent flavor is that a little goes a long way (which is good since, like all oils, it is high in calories: 120 per tablespoon). The oil contains mostly monounsaturated and polyunsaturated fats as well as some vitamin E. There is also a type of sesame oil available in health food stores that is "cold-pressed"; it, too, has the same mono- and polyunsaturated oils, but has a neutral flavor.

cook's notes: Sesame oil is most flavorful if added toward the end of cooking, as high heat breaks it down and dissipates its fragrance.

oranges

what's in it While most people tend to associate the benefits of oranges and their juice with vitamin C, they may not be aware that oranges are also a rich source of folate, potassium, fiber, and thiamin. While 1 cup of orange juice supplies 91% of the suggested daily intake for vitamin C, the whole fruit offers the added benefit of more than 3 grams of fiber.

pears

what's in it Juicy and tender, pears offer a good amount of dietary fiber, including heart-healthy pectin. In part because of their fiber content, pears make a satisfying low-calorie dessert. For example, 2 poached pear halves have less than 100 calories (if a low-calorie poaching liquid is used).

peppers, bell

what's in it Although all bell peppers provide fiber and vitamin B$_6$, there are some nutritional differences that depend on the color of the pepper. For example, yellow and red bell peppers provide more than twice the amount of vitamin C in green peppers. And red peppers contain eleven times more beta carotene than green. One large green pepper has only 44 calories.

cook's notes: To maximize the bioavailability of the carotenoids, cook peppers until they are crisp-tender, and eat with a little monounsaturated fat, such as canola or olive oil. For vitamin C, eat uncooked peppers, since this vitamin is easily destroyed by heat.

scallops

what's in it Scallops, in spite of their very rich texture and flavor, are quite low in calories—only 120 calories for 6 large sea scallops. Unlike most other shellfish, scallops are extremely low in cholesterol. They are a good low-fat source of protein and are rich in vitamin B$_{12}$, vitamin E, potassium, and magnesium. They also have small amounts of omega-3 fatty acids.

cook's notes: The vitamins and minerals in scallops are not affected by heat, but they should be cooked briefly to keep them from getting tough.

shrimp

what's in it Shrimp are low in calories (only 35 calories for about 6 medium shrimp) and saturated fat, and they supply protein, niacin, vitamin B$_{12}$, vitamin D, iron, selenium, and zinc. The fat in shrimp is largely polyunsaturated, and includes heart-healthy omega-3 fatty acids.

cook's notes: The nutrients in shrimp are not adversely affected by heat, but the texture is. Brief cooking keeps the shrimp from getting tough.

squash, summer

what's in it Summer squash are extremely low in calories (about 19 per cup of raw sliced squash) but as a result have a modest amount of nutrients. Nonetheless, they have decent amounts of vitamin C (about 13% of the RDA in a cup), fiber, potassium, and magnesium. In addition, zucchini, with its edible dark green skin, is a leading source of lutein and zeaxanthin, carotenoid pigments that are important for eye health.

cook's notes: Summer squash can be eaten both raw and cooked. Raw squash (as in a vegetable slaw) will be higher in vitamin C, which is partially destroyed by heat. When cooking squash, be careful not to use too much fat (although a little bit of unsaturated fat is helpful in making the carotenoids more bioavailable), because the spongy flesh of the squash soaks up fat easily.

tomatoes

what's in it Ever-popular tomatoes supply fiber, thiamin, vitamin B$_6$, iron, potassium, and lots of vitamin C: One medium tomato will give you 66% of the RDA for vitamin C. Tomatoes—especially in cooked, condensed forms such as tomato paste, sauce, juice, ketchup, and puree—are an important source of lycopene, a carotenoid that is linked to a reduced risk of prostate cancer.

cook's notes: Lycopene levels are the highest in concentrated forms of tomatoes, such as tomato paste, juice, ketchup, sauce, and soup. The more concentrated the tomato source, the more concentrated the lycopene. Heat and oil enhance absorption of lycopene and beta carotene, though some vitamin C is lost.

turkey

what's in it Turkey is an excellent source of protein, riboflavin, niacin, vitamin B$_6$, vitamin B$_{12}$, selenium, iron, and zinc. While most of the fat in turkey is found in the skin, turkey meat is so low in fat that eating 3 ounces of roasted breast meat with skin would furnish only 130 calories, 19% of them coming from fat. The dark meat is higher in fat than the light meat, but it is still relatively lean if eaten without the skin.

cook's notes: Although less fatty than chicken, turkey skin still has a substantial amount of fat. For roasting whole turkey or turkey breast, you can leave the skin on, but remove it before eating.

recipes: a user's guide

focus on food, not numbers

The basic message, regardless of health concerns, is to eat a variety of foods, especially fruits, vegetables, and grains, with a minimum of fat (specifically saturated fat). If you follow these precepts, you probably will not have to concern yourself with fat and calorie calculations. (Note that your calorie needs are determined by a host of factors including body mass, how much you exercise on a regular basis, and such biological factors as metabolism and genetics.) However, if you are trying to keep track, the most important thing to understand is that you should be evaluating your intake not for an individual dish in a meal, and not even for the meal itself, but for a day's intake—and, ideally, for a week's intake.

nutrition analysis

Each recipe in this cookbook is accompanied by a nutritional analysis, including values for calories, total fat (with the amount of saturated fat in parenthesis), cholesterol, dietary fiber, carbohydrates, protein, and sodium. "Number crunchers" will want to use the actual values to determine their day's intake, but almost all of the recipes are designed to conform to sensible intakes of calories and fat (see "On the Menu," opposite page).

good source of

In the nutritional analysis for each recipe is a section called "good source of," which lists vitamins, minerals, and other healthful compounds. In order for a recipe to qualify as a "good source of" a nutrient, it must provide a certain percentage of the recommended daily intake for that nutrient (when there are different values for men and women—see the chart on page 153—our calculations

are based on the higher of the two). In the case of a main course dish, it must provide at least 25% of the recommended intake. Side dishes and desserts must provide between 10% and 20%, depending on their calories (the more calories a dish brings with it, the greater our expectation for its nutrient content).

leading sources

In the back of the book, on page 152, you'll find charts that list the "Leading Sources" of the nutrients featured in this book. A food makes it onto the chart by having at least 10% of the recommended intake for that nutrient (see the chart on page 153). Knowing which foods are especially high in important nutrients should help you when you are choosing foods to cook as side dishes, or even creating your own recipes.

spotlite recipes

In our "Spotlite" recipes, we focus on certain aspects of cooking that we think can make healthful eating more enjoyable or more efficient—or both. A "Spotlite" recipe can introduce a person who has an interesting contribution to make to healthful cooking, or it can focus on a healthy cooking technique, unusual ingredients, or time-saving cooking equipment. And sometimes we will take an old standby recipe and give it a health makeover. Here's what you'll find in these pages:

- **Spicy Pea Guacamole** (*page 18*), a health makeover for a favorite appetizer.
- **Tomato-Shrimp Bisque** (*page 30*), how to make a low-fat seafood cream soup.
- **Jamaican Jerked Chicken** (*page 61*), using Jamaican "jerk" spices to create a highly flavorful chicken dish.

- **Sloppy Josés** (*page 81*), an introduction to TVP (a type of soy protein).
- **Polenta with Meatless Mushroom Sauce** (*page 97*), an introduction to a great Italian cornmeal dish, polenta.
- **Kasha with Mushrooms** (*page 113*), cooking with roasted buckwheat groats, a good source of lysine and magnesium.
- **Mango & Dried Fruit Compote** (*page 124*), mangoes have a luscious texture and lots of beta carotene.
- **Cocoa Brownies** (page 129), using healthful walnut oil for flavor in brownies.
- **Pumpkin Cheesecake Puddings** (*page 134*), a delicious dessert makeover from Patrice Benneward, executive editor of *Johns Hopkins Health After 50* newsletter.
- **Pumpkin Seed Granola** (*page 145*), pumpkin seeds, oats, and wheat germ make a super-nutritious breakfast cereal.

▶ homemade recipes

These are recipes for dishes that you might ordinarily buy premade, but whose nutritional profile you can improve by making them from scratch. Some of the recipes can be put together on a weekend, when you have more time, and then stored in the refrigerator or freezer for future use. In this book, the homemade recipes are:

- **Broths** (*page 25*), including a chicken broth made with carrot juice, a flavorful fresh herb broth, and an onion broth.
- **Fresh Salsas** (*page 69*), spicy fruit and vegetable relishes to perk up the meal.
- **Savory Shakes** (*page 108*), a collection of super-healthy snacks.
- **Fat-Free Dressings** (*page 119*), tricks for making delicious salad dressings with no fat.
- **Pancakes Mixes** (*page 140*), you can't beat the nutritional profile of these homemade mixes.

▶ off-the-shelf recipes

With these recipes we try to take advantage of convenient packaged foods without compromising the healthful nature of the dish. Since cooking from scratch takes time and fast food is often bad for your health, we've tried to find a satisfying middle ground.

▶ in the margins

On most recipe pages, you'll find tips that fall into one of the following categories:

F.Y.I. This is additional information on an ingredient in a dish or the nutrient content of a dish. For example, if the nutrition analysis tells you that the dish is a "good source of" folate, the F.Y.I. will explain which ingredients are providing the folate, and also remind you what folate is good for.

ON THE *Menu* If the fat or calories in an individual dish are a bit high, On the Menu will suggest other dishes that will create a well-rounded meal and also keep the overall fat percentage for that meal at a reasonable level. It's important to understand that a dish should fit into the context of a full meal and not be evaluated on its own.

KITCHEN *tip* Kitchen tips are, as the title suggests, information of value to the cook: how to shop for certain ingredients, short-cuts to make the recipe easier, or an explanation of a technique used in the recipe.

Mexican-Style Grilled Shrimp Cocktail

If you want to have more shrimp to go around, you could make this with medium instead of large shrimp. The downside is that it will take more time to shell and devein them.

> 2 tablespoons fresh lime juice
> 1 teaspoon cumin
> 1½ teaspoons chili powder
> ½ cup no-salt-added ketchup
> 2 tablespoons chopped cilantro
> 1 teaspoon ground coriander
> 1 pound large shrimp (about 24), shelled and deveined

1 In a small bowl, combine 1 tablespoon of the lime juice, ½ teaspoon of the cumin, the chili powder, ketchup, and cilantro. Stir to blend. Cover and refrigerate.

2 Preheat the broiler. Spray a broiler pan with nonstick cooking spray.

3 In a large bowl, combine the remaining 1 tablespoon lime juice, ½ teaspoon cumin, and the ground coriander. Add the shrimp, tossing to coat. Broil the shrimp 4 to 6 inches from the heat for 3 minutes, turning them over midway, until firm and pink. Let cool to room temperature.

4 Transfer the shrimp to a medium bowl. Cover and refrigerate until well chilled, about 30 minutes. Serve with the sauce. ***Makes 4 servings***

F.Y.I.

The tiny, round, yellow-tan seeds of the coriander plant have no flavor resemblance to the plant's leaves (which are commonly called cilantro). Coriander comes both as whole seeds and ground. Pungently spicy, yet sweet and slightly fruity (like an orange), coriander is a key component in curries and is often used in spice cakes and cookies.

Chili-Lime Corn Chips

These spicy chips would be the perfect accompaniment to Spicy Pea Guacamole (*page 18*).

> ¼ cup fresh lime juice
> 2 teaspoons chili powder
> ½ teaspoon coriander
> ¼ teaspoon salt
> 8 corn tortillas (6 inches), each cut into 6 wedges

1 Preheat the oven to 400°F. Spray 2 large baking sheets with nonstick cooking spray.

2 In a small bowl, whisk together the lime juice, chili powder, coriander, and salt. Dip the tortillas wedges into the lime mixture.

3 Place the tortilla wedges on the baking sheets and bake 8 to 10 minutes, or until lightly browned, turning them over halfway through the baking time. Transfer the chips to a wire rack to cool. ***Makes 4 servings***

Lemon-Curry Corn Chips Substitute fresh lemon juice for the lime juice. Use 2 teaspoons curry powder instead of chili powder. The coriander and salt remain the same.

Spotlite recipe

Spicy Pea Guacamole

2 packages (10 ounces each) frozen peas, thawed
2 tablespoons fresh lime juice
2 tablespoons reduced-fat sour cream
1 pickled jalapeño pepper
½ teaspoon salt
1 small red onion, finely chopped
½ cup chopped cilantro

1 In a food processor, combine the peas, lime juice, sour cream, jalapeño, and salt, and puree until smooth.

2 Transfer to a serving bowl and stir in the red onion and cilantro. *Makes 8 servings*

PER SERVING **66 calories, 0.6g total fat (0.3g saturated), 1mg cholesterol, 4g dietary fiber, 11g carbohydrate, 4g protein, 237mg sodium**
Good source of: **folate, thiamin, vitamin C**

Spiced Caribbean Pumpkin Soup

This flavorful tropical soup is equally delicious served warm, at room temperature, or well chilled.

1½ teaspoons cumin
¼ teaspoon black pepper
¼ teaspoon nutmeg
⅛ teaspoon allspice
Pinch of cayenne pepper
1½ teaspoons olive oil
1 medium onion, coarsely chopped
1 clove garlic, minced
1¾ cups water
½ teaspoon salt
1½ cups canned unsweetened pumpkin puree
2 tablespoons honey
1 tablespoon fresh lime juice
¼ cup plain fat-free yogurt (optional)
Lime wedges, for serving

1 In a small bowl, mix the cumin, black pepper, nutmeg, allspice, and cayenne. In a medium nonstick saucepan, heat the oil over medium heat. Add the spices and cook, stirring, for 30 seconds to release the flavors.

2 Add the onion and garlic, stirring to combine. Add the water and salt. Cover and bring to a boil. Reduce the heat to medium-low and simmer 5 minutes.

3 Whisk in the pumpkin. Bring to a simmer, cover, and cook over low heat, stirring occasionally, for 15 minutes to blend the flavors.

4 Remove from the heat and stir in the honey and lime juice. Serve the soup topped with a dollop of yogurt (if using) and with lime wedges for squeezing. *Makes 4 servings*

KITCHEN *tip*

Spray the measuring spoon (or cup) lightly with nonstick cooking spray before measuring out honey (or any other thick syrup, such as molasses). This light coating allows all the honey to flow easily out of the spoon or cup.

Creamy Carrot & Rice Soup

Leeks are generally quite sandy and need to be washed before using. Trim the root end and the tough, dark-green leaves from the leeks. Then slice the leeks crosswise and place the slices in a big bowl of lukewarm water. Swish them around vigorously in the water and let stand for several minutes; the dirt will settle to the bottom of the bowl. With your fingers, lift the leeks out of the water. If they are particularly dirty, repeat the process, using fresh water.

per serving	
calories	193
total fat	0.9g
saturated fat	0.3g
cholesterol	1mg
dietary fiber	4g
carbohydrate	42g
protein	5g
sodium	359mg

good source of:
beta carotene, folate, potassium, thiamin, vitamin B₆, vitamin C

½ cup rice
2½ cups sliced carrots
1 large leek, sliced (about 2 cups)
1 large onion, sliced
1 clove garlic, peeled
One ¼-inch slice fresh ginger, peeled
1 cup carrot juice
½ teaspoon salt
¼ teaspoon pepper
1 cup water
½ cup low-fat (1%) milk
2 tablespoons minced fresh dill

1 In a medium saucepan, cook the rice according to package directions, but omitting the salt. Remove from the heat.

2 Meanwhile, in a large saucepan, combine the carrots, leek, onion, garlic, ginger, carrot juice, salt, pepper, and water. Cover and bring to a boil over high heat. Reduce the heat to medium and simmer until the vegetables are very tender, about 10 minutes.

3 In a food processor or blender, puree the soup along with half the rice until smooth. Return to the large saucepan, stir in the milk and heat over medium heat.

4 Scoop the remaining rice into soup bowls, ladle the soup on top, and sprinkle with the dill. *Makes 4 servings*

Carrot & Barley Soup with Basil Use barley instead of rice and substitute fresh basil for the dill.

Off-the-Shelf

Here's a really sneaky way to take a canned soup and turn it into a luscious, creamy chowder: Just add some instant mashed potato flakes and frozen vegetables. The potatoes thicken the soup without adding any fat, and the vegetables provide the chunky chowder-like texture. The lemon zest and tarragon give a fresh, herbal flavor to the canned soup. The whole thing shouldn't take more than 15 minutes to pull together. Serve the chowder with whole-grain toast and a tossed green salad.

Tomato-Vegetable Chowder

¼ cup instant mashed potato flakes
½ cup water
1 can (10¾ ounces) reduced-fat, reduced-sodium
   tomato soup
1 teaspoon grated lemon zest
½ teaspoon tarragon
½ teaspoon black pepper
¼ teaspoon salt
1 cup frozen peas
1 cup frozen corn kernels
½ cup jarred roasted red peppers, diced
⅔ cup low-fat (1%) milk

1 In a medium saucepan, whisk the potato flakes into the water and cook over low heat until smooth.

2 Stir in the tomato soup, lemon zest, tarragon, black pepper, and salt. Add the peas, corn, and roasted red peppers, and simmer until heated through, about 4 minutes.

3 Stir in the milk and cook just until heated through, about 1 minute. *Makes 4 servings*

PER SERVING 130 calories, 1.5g total fat (0.5g saturated), 2mg cholesterol, 3g dietary fiber, 25g carbohydrate, 6g protein, 335mg sodium
Good source of: **folate, niacin, riboflavin, thiamin, vitamin C**

Green & Orange Minestrone

In a classic Italian minestrone, the pasta used would most likely be ditalini or small elbows, but we've used alphabets just for fun. Any small soup pasta should cook in about the same amount of time.

2 teaspoons olive oil
1 large onion, chopped
3 cloves garlic, minced
1 cup diced carrots
2 packages (10 ounces each) frozen chopped spinach, thawed
¾ teaspoon salt
¾ teaspoon oregano
2½ cups water
½ cup alphabet pasta
1 cup canned chick-peas, rinsed and drained
1 cup diced plum tomatoes
⅓ cup chopped fresh basil
1 tablespoon plus 1 teaspoon grated Parmesan cheese (optional)

1 In a large nonstick skillet, heat the oil over medium-high heat. Add the onion and garlic, and cook 1 minute.

2 Stir in the carrots and cook 2 minutes.

3 Add the spinach, salt, and oregano, and stir to coat. Stir in the water and bring to a boil. Stir in the pasta and cook until tender, about 5 minutes.

4 Add the chick-peas and tomatoes, and cook just until heated through. Stir the fresh basil into the soup. Serve sprinkled with the Parmesan (if using). **Makes 4 servings**

F.Y.I.

Soup pastas are tiny pasta shapes that are used primarily in soups (as opposed to being tossed with a sauce). In addition to the alphabet pasta called for here, there are a number of different soup pastas with interesting Italian names: *acini di pepe* (peppercorns), *semi di melone* (melon seeds), *stelline* (tiny stars), *orzo* (barley), *ditalini* (little thimbles), *anelli* (rings), *riso* (rice), and *farfalline* (little butterflies).

Garden-Fresh Gazpacho with Mint

This quick and easy variation on the classic Spanish soup from Andalusia needs a few hours of chilling time. Vine-ripened beefsteak tomatoes fresh from the garden make this an even better soup.

2 pounds tomatoes, preferably beefsteak
2 large red bell peppers, cut into large chunks
1 large green bell pepper, cut into large chunks
1/3 cup coarsely chopped sweet red or white onion
1 jalapeño pepper, seeded and coarsely chopped
2 cloves garlic, peeled
1 can (5 1/2 ounces) tomato-vegetable juice
2 tablespoons fresh lemon juice
1 tablespoon extra-virgin olive oil
1 tablespoon red wine vinegar
1/2 teaspoon salt
1/4 teaspoon black pepper
1 1/4 cups shredded carrots
1/3 cup chopped fresh mint

1 Bring a medium saucepan of water to a boil over high heat. One at a time, add the tomatoes and blanch 10 to 20 seconds to loosen the skins. Cool under cold running water and slip off the skins. Cut the tomatoes into big chunks.

2 In a food processor, combine the bell peppers, onion, jalapeño pepper, and garlic, and process until coarsely chopped. Remove about half of the mixture and transfer to a large bowl.

3 To the mixture remaining in the food processor, add the tomatoes, in batches if necessary, and process until the gazpacho is finely chopped but still has some texture. Add to the mixture in the bowl.

4 Stir in the tomato-vegetable juice, lemon juice, oil, vinegar, salt, and black pepper. Cover and chill until cold.

5 In a small bowl, mix the carrots and mint. Ladle the gazpacho into bowls and serve topped with some of the carrot-mint mixture. *Makes 6 servings*

Roasted Pepper & Black Bean Soup

The flavors of the Southwest are combined in this hearty soup, spicy with cayenne and black pepper.

¼ cup finely chopped cilantro
¼ cup reduced-fat sour cream
5 large red bell peppers, cut lengthwise into flat panels
1½ teaspoons olive oil
2 large onions, thinly sliced
3 cloves garlic, minced
¾ teaspoon salt
¼ teaspoon black pepper
¼ teaspoon cayenne pepper
2½ cups water
1 can (10½ ounces) black beans, rinsed and drained

1 Preheat the broiler.

2 Meanwhile, in a small bowl, stir together the cilantro and sour cream. Transfer to a bowl and chill until serving time.

3 Place the bell pepper pieces, skin-side up, on a broiler pan and broil 4 inches from the heat for 12 minutes or until the skin is blackened. When the peppers are cool enough to handle, peel them.

4 In a nonstick Dutch oven, heat the oil over medium-high heat. Stir in the onions, garlic, salt, black pepper, and cayenne, and sauté until the onions are softened slightly, about 2 minutes.

5 Add the bell peppers and water to the pan. Cover and bring to a boil. Reduce the heat to medium-low and simmer until the peppers and onions are very tender, about 10 minutes.

6 In a food processor or blender, puree the soup. Return the puree to the saucepan. Add the beans and cook over medium heat until warmed through. Serve the soup topped with the cilantro cream. ***Makes 6 servings***

Yellow Pepper & Chick-Pea Soup In step 1, use finely chopped fresh basil instead of cilantro. Substitute yellow bell peppers for the red peppers, and canned chick-peas (rinsed and drained) for the black beans.

HOMEMADE
broths

Making homemade broths allows you to control sodium and fat levels, and also gives you the opportunity to create some interesting flavor combinations. The Green Herb Broth will be of particular interest to anyone with a kitchen herb garden. And in our Chicken Broth, we've used carrot juice to introduce a healthful component (beta carotene) not found in storebought broths.

Green Herb Broth

2 cups packed basil leaves

2 cups packed cilantro leaves and stems

1 bunch scallions, thickly sliced

3 slices (½ inch thick) fresh ginger

4 cloves garlic, peeled and smashed

3 strips of lime zest

¼ teaspoon salt

8 cups water

In a large saucepan or stockpot, combine all the ingredients and bring to a boil over medium heat. Reduce to a simmer, partially cover, and cook until the broth is flavorful, about 45 minutes. Strain and discard the solids. Keep refrigerated. *Makes 6 cups*

PER ½ CUP: 11 CALORIES, 0.1G TOTAL FAT (0G SATURATED), 0MG CHOLESTEROL, 1G DIETARY FIBER, 2G CARBOHYDRATE, 1G PROTEIN, 56MG SODIUM

Chicken Broth

6 pounds whole chicken legs

8½ cups water

4 cups carrot juice

1 cup low-sodium tomato-vegetable juice

2 large onions, unpeeled, halved

2 large carrots, thickly sliced

1 large leek, thinly sliced

2 stalks celery, thinly sliced

8 cloves garlic, unpeeled

¾ teaspoon rosemary

¾ teaspoon thyme

10 sprigs of parsley

2 bay leaves

1 Preheat the oven to 450°F. Spread the chicken in a roasting pan and roast until browned and crisp, about 30 minutes.
2 Transfer the chicken to a large stockpot. Pour off all the fat from the roasting pan and add ½ cup of water to the pan, scraping up any browned bits. Add these juices to the stockpot with the chicken.
3 Add the remaining 8 cups water, carrot juice and mixed vegetable juice, and bring to a boil over high heat, skimming off any foam as it rises to the surface. Continue skimming until no foam remains.
4 Add the onions, carrots, leek, celery, garlic, rosemary, thyme, parsley, and bay leaves. Return to a boil, continuing to skim any foam that rises. Reduce the heat to low and simmer until the broth is rich and flavorful, about 2 hours.

5 Strain and discard the solids. Refrigerate and remove the fat that solidifies on the surface. Refrigerate for up to 3 days or freeze for longer storage. *Makes about 7 cups*

PER ½ CUP: 56 CALORIES, 2.5G TOTAL FAT (0.6G SATURATED), 3MG CHOLESTEROL, 1G DIETARY FIBER, 7G CARBOHYDRATE, 1G PROTEIN, 46MG SODIUM. **GOOD SOURCE OF:** BETA CAROTENE

Onion Broth

2 pounds Spanish onions, unpeeled and halved

2 leeks, halved lengthwise and thinly sliced

3 cloves garlic, unpeeled and halved

1 stalk celery, thinly sliced

5 sprigs of parsley

¼ teaspoon salt

8 cups water

In a large saucepan or stockpot, combine all of the ingredients and bring to a boil over high heat. Reduce to a simmer, partially cover, and cook until the broth is flavorful, about 45 minutes. Strain and discard the solids. Keep refrigerated. *Makes 6 cups*

PER ½ CUP: 42 CALORIES, 0.2G TOTAL FAT (0G SATURATED), 0MG CHOLESTEROL, 1G DIETARY FIBER, 10G CARBOHYDRATE, 1G PROTEIN, 56MG SODIUM

Apple-Winter Squash Soup

Applesauce gives this soup a satisfying thickness without adding fat. For a vegetarian soup, use Onion Broth (*page 25*) or water instead of chicken broth, and add another ¼ teaspoon salt.

1 large red bell pepper, cut lengthwise into flat panels
1 tablespoon olive oil
2 medium yellow onions, thinly sliced
2 cloves garlic, minced
1 cup unsweetened applesauce
1 package (12 ounces) frozen winter squash puree
1 cup chicken broth, homemade (*page 25*) or
    reduced-sodium canned
1 teaspoon curry powder
½ teaspoon salt
½ teaspoon black pepper
1 Granny Smith apple, minced
1 small red onion, minced

1 Preheat the broiler. Place the bell pepper pieces, skin-side up, on a broiler pan and broil 4 inches from the heat for 12 minutes or until the skin is blackened. When the peppers are cool enough to handle, peel them.

2 Meanwhile, in a medium saucepan, heat the oil over medium heat. Add the yellow onions and garlic, and cook, stirring, until the onions are light golden, 5 to 7 minutes. Add the roasted peppers and stir until coated.

3 Transfer the sautéed vegetables to a food processor and process until pureed. Add the applesauce and process just until combined.

4 Return the puree to the saucepan. Add the winter squash, broth, curry powder, salt, and black pepper, and bring to a boil over medium heat. Reduce to a simmer, cover, and cook, stirring occasionally, until the squash has thawed and the soup is piping hot, about 12 minutes.

5 In a small bowl, stir together the minced apple and red onion. Serve the soup topped with some of the apple-onion garnish. ***Makes 4 servings***

F.Y.I.

Apples are a good source of the cholesterol-lowering soluble fiber called pectin. Pectin is helpful in creating feelings of fullness by forming a viscous gel in the intestines, which slows the emptying of the stomach. You'll get more pectin from cooked apples because the pectin is released when the apples' cell walls soften as they cook. Pectin is used commercially as a thickening agent in jams, jellies, and preserves.

Mushroom, Root Vegetable & Barley Soup

Earthy root vegetables and mushrooms give this soup its rich flavor without any meat.

<table>
<tr><td colspan="2">per serving</td></tr>
<tr><td>calories</td><td>242</td></tr>
<tr><td>total fat</td><td>4.1g</td></tr>
<tr><td>saturated fat</td><td>0.6g</td></tr>
<tr><td>cholesterol</td><td>0mg</td></tr>
<tr><td>dietary fiber</td><td>6g</td></tr>
<tr><td>carbohydrate</td><td>47g</td></tr>
<tr><td>protein</td><td>6g</td></tr>
<tr><td>sodium</td><td>486mg</td></tr>
</table>

good source of: beta carotene, fiber, potassium, vitamin B$_6$, vitamin C, vitamin E

1 tablespoon olive oil
1 onion, finely chopped
3 cloves garlic, minced
3 carrots, halved and thinly sliced
2 parsnips (5 ounces each), halved and thinly sliced
1 sweet potato (8 ounces), peeled and cut into ½-inch chunks
½ pound mushrooms, thickly sliced
1 cup canned crushed tomatoes
¾ teaspoon salt
½ teaspoon rosemary, minced
6 cups water
⅓ cup quick-cooking barley

1 In a large saucepan or Dutch oven, heat the oil over medium heat. Add the onion and garlic, and cook, stirring frequently, until the onion is lightly browned, about 7 minutes.

2 Add the carrots, parsnips, and sweet potato, and cook, stirring frequently, until the carrots are crisp-tender, about 5 minutes. Add the mushrooms and cook until they begin to soften, about 3 minutes.

3 Stir in the tomatoes, salt, rosemary, and water, and bring to a boil. Add the barley, reduce the heat to a simmer, cover, and cook until the barley is tender, about 15 minutes. *Makes 4 servings*

Curried Split Pea & Mushroom Soup

Dried shiitake mushrooms give this vegetarian soup a full-bodied, meaty flavor. If you want to splurge, use dried porcini mushrooms instead.

½ cup dried shiitake mushrooms (½ ounce)
1 cup boiling water
2 teaspoons olive oil
1 large onion, finely chopped
3 cloves garlic, minced
1 red bell pepper, diced
3 cups water
¾ cup yellow or green split peas
3 tablespoons tomato paste
2 teaspoons curry powder
1 teaspoon salt
½ teaspoon black pepper

F.Y.I.

Green split peas are used in the U.S. more than yellow split peas, which are favored in Europe. Rich in flavor, texture, and fiber, split peas provide folate, potassium, thiamin, and iron.

1 In a small heatproof bowl, combine the dried mushrooms and the boiling water, and let stand for 20 minutes or until softened. Reserving the soaking liquid, scoop out the dried mushrooms and coarsely chop them. Strain the soaking liquid through a coffee filter or a paper towel-lined sieve.

2 In a large nonstick saucepan, heat the oil over medium heat. Add the onion and garlic, and cook, stirring frequently, until the onion is golden brown, about 7 minutes. Add the bell pepper and mushrooms, and cook until the pepper is tender, about 5 minutes.

3 Stir in the reserved mushroom soaking liquid, the water, split peas, tomato paste, curry powder, salt, and black pepper, and bring to a boil. Reduce to a simmer, cover, and cook until the split peas are tender, about 35 minutes.
Makes 4 servings

Spinach & Lemon Soup

Fresh with the tang of lemon, this spinach soup is a low-cholesterol, vegetarian version of the traditional Greek *avgolemono* soup. It's delicious served with toasted pita triangles.

per serving	
calories	160
total fat	1.9g
saturated fat	0.5g
cholesterol	53mg
dietary fiber	5g
carbohydrate	30g
protein	8g
sodium	560mg

good source of: beta carotene, fiber, folate, magnesium, potassium, riboflavin, selenium, thiamin, vitamin B_6, vitamin C, vitamin E

4 cups water
½ cup rice
1 medium onion, finely chopped
2 cloves garlic, minced
1 teaspoon oregano
¾ teaspoon salt
¼ teaspoon pepper
1 teaspoon grated lemon zest
1 cup shredded carrots
8 cups loosely packed spinach leaves, cut into
   1-inch-wide strips
1 large egg
1 large egg white
¼ cup fresh lemon juice

1 In a Dutch oven or flameproof casserole, combine the water, rice, onion, garlic, oregano, salt, pepper, and lemon zest. Cover and bring to a boil over high heat. Reduce the heat to low and simmer until the rice is very tender, about 20 minutes.

2 Stir in the carrots and cook 5 minutes. Stir in the spinach and increase the heat to medium. Cook uncovered, stirring constantly, just until the spinach is wilted, 2 to 3 minutes.

3 In a small bowl, whisk together the whole egg, egg white, and 1 tablespoon water. Whisk in a spoonful of the hot soup to warm the eggs. Stirring constantly, pour the warmed egg mixture into the soup. As soon as all of the egg has been added, remove the soup from the heat.

4 Stir in the lemon juice and serve hot. ***Makes 4 servings***

Spotlite recipe

Tomato-Shrimp Bisque

A bisque is a smooth, thick seafood soup, usually enriched with heavy cream. Here, potatoes help give a sense of richness without adding fat. If you don't have an immersion blender, you could puree this in batches in a regular blender or food processor.

2 teaspoons olive oil
1 medium onion, thinly sliced
2 carrots, thinly sliced
2 tablespoons minced fresh ginger
3 cloves garlic, minced
2 cups water
1 baking potato (8 ounces), peeled and thinly sliced
1 teaspoon grated lemon zest
1 teaspoon tarragon
¾ teaspoon salt
1 pound medium shrimp, shelled and deveined
1 can (14½ ounces) stewed tomatoes

1 In a large saucepan, heat the oil over low heat. Add the onion, carrots, ginger, and garlic, and cook until the onion is tender, about 7 minutes.

2 Add the water, potato, lemon zest, tarragon, and salt to the sautéed vegetables and bring to a boil. Reduce to a simmer, cover, and cook until the potato is tender, about 5 minutes.

3 Meanwhile, cut the shrimp into small pieces and set aside.

4 Add the tomatoes to the pan and return to a boil. Add the shrimp and cook until just cooked through, about 2 minutes.

5 Remove from the heat and with an immersion blender, puree the soup in the pan until thick, but not quite smooth. *Makes 4 servings*

PER SERVING 234 calories, 4.5g total fat (0.7g saturated), 162mg cholesterol, 4g dietary fiber, 25g carbohydrate, 24g protein, 837mg sodium
Good source of: beta carotene, magnesium, niacin, omega-3 fatty acids, potassium, selenium, thiamin, vitamin B_{12}, vitamin B_6, vitamin C, vitamin D, zinc

per serving	
calories	194
total fat	2.9g
saturated fat	0.6g
cholesterol	75mg
dietary fiber	5g
carbohydrate	21g
protein	8g
sodium	396mg

good source of: beta carotene, niacin, omega-3 fatty acids, potassium, selenium, vitamin B_{12}, vitamin B_6, vitamin C

Oven-Steamed Bass with Thai-Style Vegetables

Certainly for those who will partake of it, as well as for the person who prepared it, there is an undeniable thrill that comes when a whole cooked fish, fragrant and beautifully garnished, arrives at the dinner table.

¼ cup water
4 cloves garlic, peeled
2 tablespoons coarsely chopped fresh ginger
1 tablespoon reduced-sodium soy sauce
1 tablespoon honey
1 tablespoon rice wine vinegar
4 anchovy fillets or 1½ tablespoons anchovy paste
2 cups small broccoli florets
4 large carrots, cut into long, slender sticks
8 scallions, cut into 2-inch lengths
½ pound fresh shiitake mushrooms, stems discarded and
    caps cut into ½-inch slices
2 large jalapeño peppers, cut into thin slivers
2 whole black bass or striped bass (1 pound each)
½ cup cilantro sprigs, for garnish

1 Preheat the oven to 450°F.

2 Place the water, garlic, ginger, soy sauce, honey, vinegar and anchovies in a food processor. Process until the ingredients are finely minced.

3 In the bottom of a broiler pan or in a large roasting pan, place the broccoli, carrots, scallions, mushrooms, and jalapeño peppers. Toss to combine the ingredients and then drizzle with half of the soy sauce mixture.

4 Place the fish on top of the vegetables and drizzle with the remaining soy sauce mixture. Cover with foil and bake 25 to 30 minutes, or until the fish just flakes when tested with a fork.

5 Transfer the fish, vegetables, and cooking juices to a heated platter. Garnish with the cilantro sprigs. ***Makes 4 servings***

Italian-Style Monkfish Stir-Fry

Stir-fries needn't be restricted to Asian dishes. Here, monkfish is stir-fried with sun-dried tomatoes, broccoli, and pine nuts for a distinctly Italian dish. Monkfish, more and more available these days, holds up superbly to the rigors of stir-frying because of its firm flesh.

¼ cup sun-dried tomatoes (not oil-packed)
½ cup boiling water
2 teaspoons olive oil
3 tablespoons chopped Canadian bacon (1 ounce)
2 teaspoons pine nuts
1½ pounds boneless monkfish, cut into ½-inch chunks
1 tablespoon flour
¼ cup minced scallions
3 cloves garlic, minced
3 cups small broccoli florets
¼ cup golden raisins
¼ cup orange juice

1 In a small heatproof bowl, combine the sun-dried tomatoes and boiling water. Let stand until the tomatoes have softened, 15 to 20 minutes (depending on the dryness of the tomatoes). Drain, reserving the soaking liquid, and coarsely chop the tomatoes.

2 In a large nonstick skillet, heat the oil over medium heat. Add the Canadian bacon and pine nuts, and cook, stirring, for 1 minute.

3 Dust the monkfish with the flour. Add the fish to the pan and cook, turning occasionally, until golden, about 3 minutes.

4 Stir in the scallions and garlic, and cook 30 seconds. Add the broccoli, sun-dried tomatoes, reserved soaking liquid, and raisins. Cook, stirring frequently, until the fish and broccoli are tender, 4 to 5 minutes.

5 Remove the pan from the heat and stir in the orange juice. Serve hot.
Makes 4 servings

per serving	
calories	242
total fat	6.5g
saturated fat	1.2g
cholesterol	46mg
dietary fiber	3g
carbohydrate	17g
protein	29g
sodium	218mg

good source of: niacin, potassium, selenium, vitamin B_{12}, vitamin B_6, vitamin C

KITCHEN *tip*

Monkfish is sold cut into thick rounds with a center bone, or in boneless chunks. Both cuts can come with a tough, inedible membrane attached that should be removed before the fish is cooked. If you don't do this, the membrane will tighten around the piece of fish and keep the fish from cooking properly. Slip a small, sharp paring knife between the membrane and the flesh and slide the knife along the edges of the fish to pare off the membrane.

Vegetable-Topped Baked Haddock

per serving	
calories	215
total fat	5g
saturated fat	0.7g
cholesterol	82mg
dietary fiber	4g
carbohydrate	13g
protein	30g
sodium	641mg

good source of: beta carotene, magnesium, niacin, potassium, selenium, vitamin B_{12}, vitamin B_6, vitamin C, vitamin E, vitamin K

To bake fish is often to risk drying it out. In this recipe, the problem is solved by layering the fish between a bed of Swiss chard and an aromatic topping of tomatoes and herbs. You could substitute spinach or collard greens for the Swiss chard.

1 pound Swiss chard
¼ cup water
1¼ pounds haddock fillets, cut into 2-inch chunks
½ teaspoon salt
¼ teaspoon pepper
1 tablespoon olive oil
2 tomatoes, seeded, cubed, and drained
1 large onion, cut into narrow wedges
½ cup minced parsley
2 tablespoons sliced garlic
1 teaspoon tarragon

1 Preheat the oven to 450°F.

2 Separate the stems from the Swiss chard leaves. Slice the stems crosswise and set aside. Shred the leaves and place in shallow 2-quart baking dish. Sprinkle the water on top.

3 Place the fish on top of the chard and sprinkle with ¼ teaspoon of the salt and the pepper.

4 In a large nonstick skillet, heat the oil over medium-high heat. Add the chard stems, tomatoes, onion, parsley, garlic, tarragon, and the remaining ¼ teaspoon salt. Cook until the onion is crisp-tender, about 4 minutes.

5 Spoon the sautéed vegetables over the fish. Cover the dish and bake for 10 to 15 minutes, or until the fish just flakes when tested with a fork. ***Makes 4 servings***

KITCHEN *tip*

To cut carrots into matchsticks (also called julienne), cut a peeled carrot into 2-inch lengths. Then cut the 2-inch pieces lengthwise into ¼-inch-thick slices. Stack several of the slices up and cut them lengthwise into strips that are about ¼ inch wide.

Pasta with Spicy Garlic-Shrimp Sauce

Garlic-infused shrimp are pureed, then blended with sour cream, mild green chilies, and fresh basil to form a superb, one-of-a-kind sauce for pasta.

⅔ cup chicken broth, homemade (*page 25*) or reduced-sodium canned, or Green Herb Broth (*page 25*)
16 medium shrimp, unshelled
2 cloves garlic, peeled
⅓ cup reduced-fat sour cream
¼ cup chopped fresh basil
½ teaspoon salt
8 ounces bow-tie pasta
1½ cups carrot matchsticks
2 teaspoons olive oil
1 medium onion, finely chopped
1 can (4 ounces) chopped mild green chilies, drained
Lemon wedges, for serving

1 In a medium saucepan, bring the broth to a boil over medium-high heat. Add the shrimp and garlic, and return to a boil. Cover, reduce the heat to medium, and simmer until the shrimp are opaque throughout, about 2 minutes. Reserving the cooking liquid, transfer the shrimp and garlic to a plate and set aside until cool enough to handle. Measure out ⅓ cup of the cooking liquid and set aside; discard the remaining liquid.

2 Shell and devein the shrimp, then place them in a food processor and process to a paste. Add the sour cream, cooked garlic, and reserved cooking liquid, and process to a smooth puree. Stir in 2 tablespoons of the basil and the salt, and set the sauce aside.

3 In a large pot of boiling water, cook the pasta according to package directions. About 2 minutes before the pasta is done, add the carrot matchsticks.

4 Meanwhile, in a small nonstick skillet, heat the oil over medium-high heat. Add the onion and green chilies, and cook until the onion begins to soften, about 3 minutes. Stir in the shrimp sauce and the remaining 2 tablespoons basil and remove from the heat.

5 Drain the pasta and carrots in a colander and transfer to a serving bowl. Add the shrimp sauce and toss to distribute the ingredients. Serve with the lemon wedges. ***Makes 4 servings***

Off-the-Shelf

Pita breads make a convenient "crust" for individual-sized pizzas. Since it's easy and quick to throw together a pizza like this from ingredients you are likely to have on hand, consider buying extra pitas and freezing them (right in their store wrappings). Just let them come back to room temperature before you put them in the oven. Although the recipe calls for fresh broccoli, you could use frozen chopped broccoli. Thaw it and let it drain on paper towels before using.

Niçoise Pita Pizza

2 cups broccoli florets
1 cup canned cannellini beans, rinsed and drained
1 can (6 ounces) tomato paste
1 tablespoon olive oil
3 cloves garlic, minced
4 whole-wheat pitas (6 inches)
1 large red onion, halved and thinly sliced
2 cups cherry tomatoes, halved
¼ cup Calamata or other brine-cured black olives,
    pitted and coarsely chopped
1 can (6 ounces) water-packed tuna

1 Preheat the oven to 450°F. In a vegetable steamer, cook the broccoli until crisp-tender, about 3 minutes.

2 In a small bowl, with a potato masher, mash the beans with the tomato paste, oil, and garlic. Spread the mixture over the pitas. Scatter the onion on top and bake for 10 minutes.

3 Scatter the broccoli, cherry tomatoes, olives, and tuna on top and bake for 10 minutes or until the tomatoes have begun to collapse and the tuna is hot. *Makes 4 servings*

PER SERVING 413 calories, 9.1g total fat (1.4g saturated), 18mg cholesterol, 12g dietary fiber, 64g carbohydrate, 25g protein, 764mg sodium
Good source of: fiber, folate, magnesium, niacin, potassium, selenium, thiamin, vitamin B₆, vitamin C, vitamin E

Pasta Salad with Tonnato Sauce

Tonnato, or tuna sauce, is usually served over slices of cold cooked veal. The flavorful sauce makes a delightfully different pasta salad. For a stronger tuna flavor, use light tuna rather than albacore. If you like, toss in some steamed vegetables, such as broccoli florets, snow peas, or cut-up asparagus spears.

8 ounces pasta shells
1 can (6 ounces) water-packed albacore tuna, drained
½ cup reduced-fat sour cream
3 tablespoons fresh lemon juice
3 cloves garlic
¾ teaspoon black pepper
¼ teaspoon salt
2 cups sliced celery
1 large red bell pepper, diced
½ cup chopped red onion
¼ cup chopped flat-leaf parsley

1 In a large pot of boiling water, cook the pasta according to package directions. Drain, reserving ½ cup of the pasta cooking water. Rinse the pasta under cold running water and transfer to a large bowl to cool.

2 In a food processor, combine the tuna, reserved pasta cooking water, sour cream, lemon juice, garlic, pepper, and salt, and process until finely pureed.

2 Add the celery, bell pepper, onion, and parsley to the drained pasta. Add the dressing and toss to coat. Cover and refrigerate for 30 minutes. *Makes 4 servings*

Mexican Pasta Salad Tonnato In the tonnato sauce (step 2), use lime juice instead of lemon juice. Omit the black pepper and use 2 chipotle peppers packed in adobo sauce; puree them along with the other sauce ingredients.

Baked Flounder with Two Tomatoes

Fresh tomatoes and sun-drieds are combined in a smooth basil- and orange-scented sauce for baked flounder.

<table>
<tr><th colspan="2">per serving</th></tr>
<tr><td>calories</td><td>238</td></tr>
<tr><td>total fat</td><td>6.1g</td></tr>
<tr><td>saturated fat</td><td>1.7g</td></tr>
<tr><td>cholesterol</td><td>84mg</td></tr>
<tr><td>dietary fiber</td><td>3g</td></tr>
<tr><td>carbohydrate</td><td>13g</td></tr>
<tr><td>protein</td><td>33g</td></tr>
<tr><td>sodium</td><td>618mg</td></tr>
</table>

good source of:
omega-3 fatty acids, potassium, selenium, vitamin B_{12}, vitamin B_6, vitamin C, vitamin E

⅓ cup sun-dried tomatoes (not oil-packed)
1 cup boiling water
2 teaspoons olive oil
1 cup minced scallions
3 cloves garlic, minced
1½ teaspoons mild chili powder
2 cups chopped fresh tomatoes
¼ cup chopped fresh basil
2 tablespoons frozen orange juice concentrate, thawed
4 flounder fillets (6 ounces each)
½ teaspoon salt
3 tablespoons grated Parmesan cheese

KITCHEN tip

This delicate fish dish doesn't take long to cook, but does involve a certain amount of preparation. However, the two-tomato sauce can be made ahead of time. Then, about 15 minutes before serving time, preheat the oven and season the flounder. The fish takes only 7 minutes to bake.

1 Preheat the oven to 400°F. Spray a 7 x 11-inch baking dish with nonstick cooking spray.

2 In a small heatproof bowl, combine the sun-dried tomatoes and boiling water. Let stand until the tomatoes have softened, 15 to 20 minutes (depending on the dryness of the tomatoes). Drain and coarsely chop the tomatoes.

3 In a small nonstick skillet, heat the oil over medium heat. Add the scallions and garlic, and cook until the scallions are softened, about 2 minutes. Stir in the chili powder and cook until fragrant, about 1 minute.

4 In a medium bowl, combine the chopped sun-dried tomatoes, half of the scallion mixture, the fresh tomatoes, 2 tablespoons of the basil, and the orange juice concentrate. Set aside.

5 Lay the flounder on a work surface, skinned-side up. Sprinkle with the salt. Then top with the remaining scallion mixture and remaining 2 tablespoons basil. Fold the flounder over the filling and place in the baking dish in a single layer.

6 Sprinkle the fish with the Parmesan and bake for 7 minutes, or until the fish just flakes when tested with a fork. Spoon the tomato puree onto serving plates and top with the fish. ***Makes 4 servings***

Shrimp & Sweet Potato Curry

Commercial curry powders vary in strength, so if you are concerned about the spiciness of this dish, add only half the curry powder called for, taste, and then add the remainder if the dish seems too mild. If, on the other hand, you prefer hot curry, do not increase the amount of curry powder; add a bit of cayenne instead.

2 red bell peppers, cut into large pieces
½ pound unpeeled sweet potatoes, quartered
¾ cup chicken broth, homemade (*page 25*) or reduced-sodium canned
4 sun-dried tomato halves (not oil-packed)
2 teaspoons olive oil
1 cup chopped onion
2 cloves garlic, minced
2 tablespoons curry powder
½ teaspoon sugar
1 pound medium shrimp, shelled and deveined
1 green bell pepper, cut into 1-inch squares
3 tablespoons chopped cilantro
2 tablespoons nonfat sour cream

1 In a medium saucepan, bring the red bell peppers, sweet potatoes, broth, and sun-dried tomatoes to a boil over medium-high heat. Reduce the heat, cover, and simmer until the sweet potatoes are just tender, about 10 minutes.

2 Meanwhile, in a large nonstick skillet, heat the oil over medium-high heat. Add the onion and garlic, and cook, stirring, until the onion is lightly browned, about 2 minutes. Add the curry powder and cook, stirring, until the curry is fragrant, about 30 seconds. Remove the skillet from the heat.

3 Reserving the broth, transfer the cooked sweet potatoes and red bell peppers to a food processor. Add the sautéed onion mixture and process until smooth. Add the reserved broth and sugar, and process until smooth.

4 Return the sauce to the skillet and bring to a boil over medium-high heat. Add the shrimp and green bell pepper, and cook, stirring, until the shrimp are opaque throughout, 4 to 6 minutes.

5 Stir the cilantro into the curry. Serve the curry dolloped with the sour cream. ***Makes 4 servings***

Potato Pasta with Tomatoes, Peppers & Cod

The zesty flavors of Spain are at play in this dish of pasta elbows topped with tomato sauce, fresh cod, peppers, and green olives. If cod is unavailable, use scrod, haddock, or another firm-fleshed white fish. The fish's texture is important here.

per serving	
calories	365
total fat	6.4g
saturated fat	0.9g
cholesterol	61mg
dietary fiber	6g
carbohydrate	46g
protein	34g
sodium	570mg

good source of: magnesium, niacin, potassium, selenium, thiamin, vitamin B_{12}, vitamin B_6, vitamin C

1 tablespoon olive oil
¾ cup finely chopped onion
3 cloves garlic, finely chopped
1 red bell pepper, diced
2 cups chopped tomatoes
½ teaspoon grated orange zest
¼ cup orange juice
4 drops of hot pepper sauce
½ teaspoon salt
¼ teaspoon ground ginger
8 green olives, pitted and coarsely chopped
8 ounces potato pasta or wheat pasta elbows
1¼ pounds cod fillets, cut into 4 pieces
2½ teaspoons cornstarch blended with 1 tablespoon water

1 In a large nonstick skillet, heat the oil over medium-low heat. Add the onion and garlic, and cook, stirring frequently, until the onion has softened, about 7 minutes. Add the bell pepper and increase the heat to medium. Cook until the pepper has softened, about 5 minutes.

2 Stir in the tomatoes, orange zest, orange juice, hot pepper sauce, salt, and ginger. Bring to a boil, reduce to a simmer, and cook for 5 minutes to blend the flavors. Stir in the olives.

3 Meanwhile, in a large pot of boiling water, cook the pasta according to package directions. Drain.

4 Place the cod on top of the tomato-pepper mixture. Cover and cook until the fish just flakes when tested with a fork, about 10 minutes.

5 Add the cornstarch mixture to the skillet. Bring to a boil and cook until the sauce is slightly thickened, about 1 minute. Gently flake the cod with a fork. Toss with the hot pasta and serve. ***Makes 4 servings***

F.Y.I.

Potato pasta is an excellent alternative for people who are allergic to wheat or to gluten (the protein formed when wheat flour is made into batter or dough). Potato pasta is made from potato flour, which in turn is made from dried, ground-up potatoes. Potato flour has more fiber, calcium, and magnesium, and less fat, than refined semolina flour (the type used to make most wheat pastas). It also has a significant amount of potassium, since potatoes themselves are rich in this mineral. When you shop for potato pasta, be sure to buy a brand that is enriched with B vitamins.

Cod en Papillote

Except for the fresh cod, you could conceivably have all the ingredients for this quick fish dish (maybe 30 minutes prep time) sitting in your pantry. If you prefer, you can substitute salmon or tuna steaks for the cod.

1 cup no-salt-added tomato sauce
½ cup mild to medium bottled salsa
1 package (10 ounces) frozen chopped broccoli, thawed and drained
½ cup frozen corn kernels, thawed
1 tablespoon olive oil
2 cod steaks (12 ounces each), halved crosswise
2 teaspoons chili powder
½ teaspoon salt

1 Preheat the oven to 450°F. In a large bowl, combine the tomato sauce, salsa, broccoli, corn, and oil.

2 Cut four pieces of foil, 12 x 18 inches each. With the short end of the foil facing you, place the cod steaks on the bottom half of each sheet, 1 inch in from the edges. Sprinkle the cod with the chili powder and salt. Top each cod steak with the tomato-vegetable mixture.

3 Fold the foil over the vegetables and fish, folding the edges over to seal. Place the packets on a baking sheet and bake 12 minutes, or until the fish just flakes when tested with a fork. Carefully open one package (steam will escape) to check for doneness. If the fish isn't done, reseal the packet and return the baking sheet to the oven. *Makes 4 servings*

PER SERVING 229 calories, 5.2g total fat (0.8g saturated), 67mg cholesterol, 5g dietary fiber, 16g carbohydrate, 32g protein, 544mg sodium
Good source of: niacin, potassium, selenium, vitamin B$_6$, vitamin B$_{12}$, vitamin C

Spinach-Stuffed Sole

Chopped spinach has long served as a wonderful stuffing for savory dishes. In this stuffed fillet of sole dish it provides subtle flavor, beautiful color, and lots of vitamins—no mean achievement for a lone vegetable.

per serving	
calories	282
total fat	5g
saturated fat	1.4g
cholesterol	92mg
dietary fiber	4g
carbohydrate	19g
protein	41g
sodium	550mg

good source of: beta carotene, folate, magnesium, niacin, potassium, selenium, thiamin, vitamin B_{12}, vitamin B_6, vitamin C, vitamin D, vitamin E

1 large baking potato (8 ounces), peeled and thinly sliced
2 cloves garlic, peeled
½ teaspoon salt
2 tablespoons grated Parmesan cheese
⅛ teaspoon nutmeg
1 package (10 ounces) frozen chopped spinach, thawed
    and squeezed dry
4 sole fillets (6 ounces each)
4 teaspoons fresh lemon juice
1 pound plum tomatoes, thickly sliced
1 teaspoon olive oil
½ teaspoon tarragon

1 Preheat the oven to 400°F.

2 In a small saucepan, bring 2 cups of water to a boil over medium heat. Add the potato, garlic, and ⅛ teaspoon of the salt, and cook until the potato is tender, about 10 minutes.

3 With a slotted spoon, transfer the potato and garlic to a medium bowl. Measure out 2 tablespoons of the cooking liquid and add to the bowl, then mash the potato and garlic with a fork or potato masher. Stir in the Parmesan, nutmeg, and ⅛ teaspoon of the salt. Stir in the spinach.

4 Lay the sole fillets on a work surface, skinned-side up. Sprinkle 2 teaspoons of the lemon juice evenly over the fish. Spoon the spinach mixture onto the fillets and roll them up.

5 In a 7 x 11-inch baking pan, toss the tomatoes with the olive oil and remaining ¼ teaspoon salt. Place the fish rolls on top of the tomatoes, seam-side down. Sprinkle the fish with the remaining 2 teaspoons lemon juice and the tarragon. Bake 10 minutes, or until the fish just flakes when tested with a fork and the tomatoes have started to give up their juices.

6 Serve the fish rolls on a bed of the roasted tomatoes. *Makes 4 servings*

Shrimp & Pasta Salad with Orange-Parsley Dressing

You could use any type of parsley for the dressing, but flat-leaf parsley (also called Italian parsley) has more flavor than curly parsley.

per serving	
calories	242
total fat	4.9g
saturated fat	0.8g
cholesterol	161mg
dietary fiber	2g
carbohydrate	26g
protein	22g
sodium	844mg

good source of:
selenium, vitamin B$_{12}$, vitamin C, vitamin D

1 cup ditalini or small pasta shells (about 4 ounces)
1 pound medium shrimp, shelled and deveined
¾ teaspoon oregano
¾ teaspoon salt
½ cup packed parsley leaves
½ cup jarred roasted red pepper, drained
½ cup orange juice
1 tablespoon olive oil
1 cucumber, peeled, halved, seeded and thinly sliced
2 tablespoons capers, rinsed and drained

1 In a large pot of boiling water, cook the pasta according to package directions. Drain.

2 Meanwhile, preheat the broiler. Toss the shrimp with the oregano and ¼ teaspoon of the salt. Broil the shrimp 4 to 6 inches from the heat for 2 minutes per side, or until opaque throughout.

3 In a food processor, combine the remaining ½ teaspoon salt, parsley, roasted pepper, orange juice, and oil, and process until smooth. Transfer the dressing to a large bowl.

4 Add the pasta, shrimp, cucumber, and capers to the dressing, and toss to combine. Serve warm, at room temperature, or chilled. ***Makes 4 servings***

Shrimp & Barley Salad with Lemon-Cilantro Dressing Use 2/3 cup pearl barley instead of the pasta (cook according to the package directions). In the dressing (step 3), substitute lemon juice for the orange juice, but use only 2 tablespoons. Use cilantro instead of parsley. In the salad, use ¼ cup diced red onion instead of the capers.

Swordfish Milanese

In this take-off on a traditional Milanese veal dish called Veal Capricciosa (in which a veal chop is served underneath a salad), contrast is the key: The fish is hot and the salad is chilled; the fish is mild and the salad is tangy.

Swordfish:
½ teaspoon grated lemon zest
2 teaspoons fresh lemon juice
1 teaspoon olive oil
½ teaspoon rosemary, minced
½ teaspoon black pepper
¼ teaspoon salt
Pinch of cayenne pepper
4 skinned swordfish steaks (6 ounces each)

Salad:
2 tablespoons plus 2 teaspoons fresh lemon juice
4 teaspoons Dijon mustard
4 teaspoons olive oil, preferably extra-virgin
¾ teaspoon rosemary, minced
½ teaspoon salt
½ teaspoon black pepper
4 cups chopped arugula
3 cups diced plum tomatoes

1 Preheat the broiler and broiler pan or prepare the grill.

2 For the swordfish: In a small bowl, combine the lemon zest, lemon juice, oil, rosemary, black pepper, salt, and cayenne. Brush the swordfish steaks with the mixture and set aside while preparing the salad.

3 To make the salad: In a medium bowl, whisk together the lemon juice, mustard, oil, rosemary, salt, and black pepper. Add the arugula and tomatoes and toss gently to combine.

4 Broil the swordfish 2 to 3 inches from the heat, turning once, for 8 minutes, or until the fish just flakes when tested with a fork.

5 Serve the fish topped with the tomato-arugula salad. *Makes 4 servings*

per serving	
calories	236
total fat	11g
saturated fat	2.2g
cholesterol	45mg
dietary fiber	2g
carbohydrate	9g
protein	25g
sodium	685mg

good source of: niacin, omega-3 fatty acids, potassium, selenium, vitamin B_{12}, vitamin B_6, vitamin C

ON THE *Menu*

Since the swordfish is served with tomatoes and arugula, the only thing needed to round out the meal (and keep the percentage of calories from fat at a sensible level) would be a loaf of good whole-grain peasant bread.

Striped Bass Provençale

The flavors of Provence—garlic, thyme, fennel, and olives—infuse this baked fish and vegetable dish. Striped bass fillets are the fish of choice here, but could easily be replaced with sea bass. The Pernod adds an ephemeral, licorice-like taste that underscores the flavors of the fennel seeds and the fresh fennel.

per serving	
calories	267
total fat	9g
saturated fat	1.5g
cholesterol	144mg
dietary fiber	3g
carbohydrate	13g
protein	34g
sodium	412mg

good source of: magnesium, niacin, omega-3 fatty acids, potassium, selenium, vitamin B$_{12}$, vitamin B$_6$, vitamin C

2 teaspoons olive oil
3 cloves garlic, thinly sliced
1 teaspoon fennel seeds
¾ teaspoon thyme
1 large red bell pepper, cut into thin strips
1 medium red onion, halved and thinly sliced
2 cups chopped tomatoes
1 cup sliced fennel or celery
¼ cup coarsely chopped Calamata or other brine-cured
   black olives
4 skinless striped bass fillets (6 ounces each)
¼ teaspoon salt
¼ teaspoon black pepper
1 tablespoon Pernod (optional)

1 Preheat the oven to 400°F. In a 9 x 13-inch baking pan, combine the oil, garlic, fennel seeds, and thyme. Place in the oven for 5 minutes, or until fragrant.

2 Add the bell pepper and onion. Return to the oven and bake 15 minutes. Stir in the tomatoes, sliced fennel, and olives, and bake 10 minutes.

3 Place the fish on top of the vegetables, sprinkle with the salt, black pepper, and Pernod (if using). Return the pan to the oven and bake 10 minutes, or until the fish just flakes when tested with a fork. ***Makes 4 servings***

Fish Stew Arrabbiata

Arrabbiata literally means angry in Italian, but when used as part of a recipe title it means that the dish is spicy. In this simple fish stew, only the fish needs to be bought fresh. Everything else can be "off the shelf."

1 jar (16 ounces) marinara sauce
3 tablespoons frozen orange juice concentrate
¾ cup water
½ teaspoon cayenne pepper
1 can (15½ ounces) pinto beans, rinsed and drained
½ cup jarred roasted red peppers, drained and cut into
    thick strips
1 jar (6½ ounces) marinated artichoke hearts, rinsed
    and drained
1¼ pounds cod fillet, cut into 1-inch chunks

1 In a large skillet, combine the marinara sauce, orange juice concentrate, water, and cayenne.

2 Add the beans, roasted peppers, and artichoke hearts, and bring to a boil over medium heat.

3 Add the cod, reduce to a simmer, cover, and cook until the cod just flakes when tested with a fork, about 10 minutes. *Makes 4 servings*

PER SERVING 333 calories, 5.4g total fat (0.9g saturated), 61mg cholesterol, 5g dietary fiber, 38g carbohydrate, 34g protein, 884mg sodium
Good source of: fiber, folate, magnesium, niacin, omega-3 fatty acids, potassium, selenium, thiamin, vitamin B_{12}, vitamin B_6, vitamin C

Sautéed Shrimp with Garlic & Spinach

Shrimp, spinach, and garlic have natural flavor affinities. But add fresh lemon juice and roasted red peppers to the mix, and the results are irresistible. Serve in smaller portions for a first course.

per serving	
calories	161
total fat	6g
saturated fat	1g
cholesterol	135mg
dietary fiber	4g
carbohydrate	10g
protein	19g
sodium	659mg

good source of: beta carotene, folate, magnesium, omega-3 fatty acids, potassium, selenium, vitamin B_{12}, vitamin B_6, vitamin C, vitamin D

1 pound medium shrimp, shelled and deveined
1½ teaspoons grated lemon zest
1 tablespoon fresh lemon juice
½ teaspoon salt
½ teaspoon black pepper
1 tablespoon plus 1 teaspoon olive oil
6 cloves garlic, sliced
10 cups loosely packed spinach leaves
1 tablespoon water
1 cup jarred roasted red peppers, drained and
  cut into strips

On the *Menu*

Serve the shrimp and spinach dish with steamed brown rice seasoned with black pepper and some grated lemon zest. For dessert, offer blueberries topped with vanilla fat-free yogurt.

1 Toss the shrimp with the lemon zest, lemon juice, and ¼ teaspoon each of the salt and black pepper.

2 In a large deep nonstick skillet, heat the oil over high heat. Add the garlic and sauté, stirring, until golden, 2 to 3 minutes. Immediately transfer the garlic with a slotted spoon to a plate.

3 Add the shrimp to the skillet and sauté until the shrimp are just barely opaque in the center, 2 to 3 minutes. With tongs or a spoon, transfer the shrimp to a plate.

4 Add the spinach to the skillet in handfuls, adding another handful as the spinach cooks down. Drizzle the spinach with the water as it cooks. When all of the spinach has been added, season with the remaining ¼ teaspoon each salt and black pepper. Add the roasted red peppers to the skillet and cook, stirring, just until heated.

5 Return the shrimp and garlic to the skillet, and toss to mix with the spinach and peppers. ***Makes 4 servings***

Dilled Tuna Burger

Instant mashed potato flakes take the place of the breadcrumbs that are usually used to help bind a tuna burger together.

per serving	
calories	138
total fat	2.6g
saturated fat	0.7g
cholesterol	36mg
dietary fiber	0g
carbohydrate	7g
protein	21g
sodium	417mg

good source of: niacin, omega-3 fatty acids, selenium, vitamin B$_{12}$, vitamin D

⅓ cup plain fat-free yogurt
1 teaspoon grated lemon zest
2 teaspoons fresh lemon juice
¼ cup instant mashed potato flakes
2 scallions, thinly sliced
⅓ cup minced fresh dill
2 tablespoons pickle relish
2 cans (6 ounces each) water-packed albacore tuna, drained

1 In a large bowl, combine the yogurt, lemon zest, lemon juice, and mashed potato flakes, stirring until moistened.

2 Add the scallions, dill, and pickle relish, and stir until well combined. Add the tuna and combine. Shape the tuna mixture into 4 patties.

3 Preheat the broiler. Spray a broiler pan with nonstick cooking spray. Broil the tuna patties 4 to 6 inches from the heat, without turning them over, until a crust has formed and the burgers are heated through, about 8 minutes. *Makes 4 servings*

Thai Tuna Burger Use lime juice instead of lemon juice. In place of the dill, use 2 tablespoons chopped fresh mint and 3 tablespoons chopped fresh basil or cilantro.

Sautéed Scallops Niçoise

per serving	
calories	199
total fat	4.9g
saturated fat	0.6g
cholesterol	37mg
dietary fiber	1g
carbohydrate	12g
protein	20g
sodium	574mg

good source of: selenium, vitamin B_{12}

Recipes from the city of Nice in the south of France often contain olives. To be more authentic, make this sautéed scallop dish with Niçoise olives, which are small, dark brownish-purple salt-cured olives. We've called for Calamata olives, which are large Greek brine-cured olives, because they are much more available and easier to pit.

1 pound sea scallops, halved horizontally
2 tablespoons flour
2 teaspoons olive oil
1 pint cherry tomatoes, halved
3 cloves garlic, minced
⅔ cup dry white wine, homemade chicken broth (*page 25*), or Green Herb Broth (*page 25*)
⅓ cup chopped fresh basil
¼ cup Calamata olives, pitted and coarsely chopped
¼ teaspoon rosemary, minced
½ teaspoon salt
1 teaspoon cornstarch blended with 1 tablespoon cold water

1 Dredge the scallops in the flour, shaking off the excess. In a large nonstick skillet, heat the oil over medium-high heat. Add the scallops and sauté until golden brown and just barely opaque, about 1 minute per side. With a slotted spoon, transfer the scallops to a bowl.

2 Add the tomatoes and garlic to the pan and cook for 1 minute. Add the wine, basil, olives, rosemary, and salt, and bring to a boil. Add the cornstarch mixture, and cook, stirring, until slightly thickened, about 1 minute.

3 Reduce to a simmer. Return the scallops to the pan, and cook just until heated through, about 1 minute. ***Makes 4 servings***

Lemony Bulgur & Shrimp Salad

Carrot juice adds a natural sweetness to the broiled shrimp in this lemony salad, but you could use tomato juice or spicy tomato-vegetable juice.

1½ cups bulgur
2 cups boiling water
½ cup carrot juice
1 teaspoon coriander
¾ pound large shrimp, shelled and deveined
⅓ cup fresh lemon juice
2 tablespoons olive oil
2 tablespoons Dijon mustard
¾ teaspoon salt
2 cups cherry tomatoes, halved
1 cup frozen peas, thawed
1 small red onion, minced

1 In a medium heatproof bowl, combine the bulgur and boiling water. Let stand until the bulgur has softened, about 30 minutes. If any liquid remains in the bowl, drain the bulgur and squeeze it dry.

2 Meanwhile, preheat the broiler. In a large bowl, stir together the carrot juice and coriander. Add the shrimp and toss to coat. Place the shrimp on a broiler pan and broil 4 to 6 inches from the heat, turning the shrimp over once, for 3 minutes or until the shrimp are opaque throughout. When cool enough to handle, cut the shrimp into bite-size pieces.

3 In a small bowl, whisk together the lemon juice, oil, mustard, and salt. Pour the dressing over the drained bulgur and toss to combine.

4 Add the shrimp, tomatoes, peas, and red onion to the bulgur, and stir to combine. Serve at room temperature or chilled. ***Makes 4 servings***

per serving	
calories	369
total fat	9.2g
saturated fat	1.3g
cholesterol	101mg
dietary fiber	13g
carbohydrate	56g
protein	21g
sodium	807mg

good source of: fiber, magnesium, niacin, selenium, thiamin, vitamin B$_{12}$, vitamin B$_6$, vitamin C

ON THE *Menu*

This salad is a meal in itself. Nothing else is required, though you could precede the main course with vegetable crudités for dipping in store-bought salsa. End the meal with sliced fresh peaches.

F.Y.I.

Curry powder is not one spice but a blend of spices, commonly used in Indian cooking to flavor a dish with sweet heat. It also adds a characteristic yellow-orange color. While curry blends vary (consisting of as many as 20 herbs and spices), they typically include turmeric (for its vivid yellow color), fenugreek, ginger, cardamom, cloves, cumin, coriander, and cayenne pepper. Madras curry is hotter than other storebought types.

Curry-Broiled Snapper

Super-quick and easy to prepare, these fillets are delicious with a storebought chutney or a homemade fresh fruit salsa, such as Banana-Kiwi Salsa or Citrus Salsa (*both on page 69*).

2½ teaspoons curry powder
¾ teaspoon coriander
¾ teaspoon sugar
½ teaspoon salt
⅛ teaspoon pepper
4 red snapper fillets (5 ounces each), skinned
2 teaspoons olive oil

1 Preheat the broiler. In a small bowl, stir together the curry powder, coriander, sugar, salt, and pepper.

2 Rub the curry mixture into one side of the snapper fillets. Brush the fish with oil.

3 Broil the fish, curry-side up, 4 to 6 inches from heat for 5 to 7 minutes, or until it just flakes when tested with a fork. ***Makes 4 servings***

Chili-Broiled Snapper Substitute chili powder for the curry powder, and use cumin instead of coriander. Serve with Corn Salsa (*page 69*).

Spicy Shrimp Chowder

per serving	
calories	247
total fat	3.7g
saturated fat	0.6g
cholesterol	86mg
dietary fiber	4g
carbohydrate	39g
protein	15g
sodium	734mg

good source of: beta carotene, niacin, omega-3 fatty acids, potassium, riboflavin, selenium, vitamin B_{12}, vitamin B_6, vitamin C, vitamin D, vitamin E

Chowders usually have white potatoes in them, but we've substituted sweet potatoes. They are a wonderful source of beta carotene, fiber, and vitamin E.

2 teaspoons olive oil

1 green bell pepper, diced

1 medium onion, finely chopped

4 cloves garlic, minced

1 pound sweet potatoes, peeled and cut into ½-inch cubes

1½ cups water

1 cup bottled clam juice or homemade chicken broth (*page 25*)

1½ teaspoons Louisiana-style hot sauce

½ teaspoon thyme

½ teaspoon salt

1 can (14½ ounces) diced tomatoes

½ pound medium shrimp, shelled, deveined, and cut into bite-size pieces

1 In a large nonstick saucepan, heat the oil over medium heat. Add the green bell pepper, onion, and garlic, and cook until the onion is tender, about 7 minutes.

2 Stir in the sweet potatoes, water, clam juice, hot sauce, thyme, and salt, and bring to a boil. Add the tomatoes, reduce to a simmer, cover, and cook until the sweet potatoes are tender, about 10 minutes.

3 Add the shrimp. Cover and cook until the shrimp are opaque throughout, about 3 minutes. ***Makes 4 servings***

Spicy Clam Chowder Use carrot juice instead of water. Substitute 1 pickled jalapeño pepper, minced, for the hot sauce. Replace the shrimp with 1 dozen shucked littleneck clams. Add the clams in step 3 and cook for only 1 to 2 minutes.

ON THE *Menu*

Serve this braised beef with mashed potatoes and low-fat coleslaw. For dessert, offer cubes of chilled honeydew melon sprinkled with chopped fresh mint.

Soy & Ginger Braised Beef

Sherry is a fortified wine from southern Spain, but it is frequently used in Chinese-style dishes, such as this darkly spiced, sweet and savory braised beef dish.

¼ cup reduced-sodium soy sauce
¼ cup sherry
2 tablespoons packed dark brown sugar
2 tablespoons ketchup
2 tablespoons minced fresh ginger
3 scallions, thinly sliced
2 cloves garlic, minced
½ teaspoon cinnamon
1 cup water
¾ pound well-trimmed top round of beef, in one piece
2 carrots, halved lengthwise and thinly sliced crosswise
2 parsnips, halved lengthwise and thinly sliced crosswise
1 green bell pepper, cut into ½-inch chunks
1½ teaspoons cornstarch blended with 1 tablespoon water

1 In a medium saucepan, combine the soy sauce, sherry, brown sugar, ketchup, ginger, scallions, garlic, cinnamon, and 1 cup water over medium heat.

2 Add the beef, cover, and simmer for 30 minutes.

3 Add the carrots, parsnips, and bell pepper. Cover and simmer until the beef is cooked to medium, about 20 minutes.

4 Remove the beef from the pan and set aside. Bring the mixture in the pan to a boil, stir in the cornstarch mixture, and cook, stirring, until the sauce is slightly thickened, about 1 minute. Thinly slice the beef and serve topped with sauce and vegetables. ***Makes 4 servings***

Braised Pork & Root Vegetables Substitute 1 pound pork tenderloin (halved crosswise) for the beef. Add ½ pound peeled and cubed white turnips.

Pork Stew with Pears

The pears add a hint of sweetness and plenty of texture (as well as fiber) to this pork and pepper stew. The stew can be made in advance and gently reheated at serving time.

2 tablespoons flour
1 teaspoon cumin
1 pound well-trimmed pork tenderloin, cut crosswise into ¼-inch slices
1 tablespoon olive oil
2 onions, cut into 1-inch chunks
2 green Italian frying peppers, cut into 1-inch squares
3 cloves garlic, finely chopped
2 medium pears, peeled and cut into 1-inch pieces
⅓ cup dry sherry
¾ cup chicken broth, homemade (*page 25*) or reduced-sodium canned
½ teaspoon salt
½ teaspoon black pepper

1 In a medium bowl, combine the flour and cumin. Dredge the pork in the flour mixture, shaking off the excess.

2 In a nonstick Dutch oven, heat the oil over medium heat. Add the pork and cook until golden brown, about 2 minutes per side. With a slotted spoon, transfer the pork to a plate.

3 Add the onions, frying peppers, and garlic, and cook, stirring frequently, until the peppers are crisp tender, about 5 minutes.

4 Add the pears and sherry, and bring to a boil. Boil 1 minute. Add the broth, salt, and black pepper, and bring to a boil. Return the pork to the pan, reduce to a simmer, and cook until the pork is cooked through and the pears are tender, about 3 minutes. ***Makes 4 servings***

KITCHEN *tip*

Italian frying peppers are thin-skinned and sweet (as opposed to hot). If you can't find them, use regular green bell peppers instead.

Classic Fajitas

You don't have to use sweet onions here, but they do caramelize more easily than other onions, adding a wonderful depth of flavor to the fajitas. If you'd like, you can also serve salsa to wrap up in the tortillas with the other ingredients.

1 tablespoon chili powder
1 teaspoon oregano
1 teaspoon sugar
½ teaspoon salt
2 large sweet onions (such as Vidalia), halved and
    thickly sliced
1 red bell pepper, cut lengthwise into flat panels
1 yellow bell pepper, cut lengthwise into flat panels
¾ pound flank steak
2 tablespoons fresh lime juice
8 low-fat flour tortillas (6 inches)
½ cup plain fat-free yogurt

1 Preheat the broiler. In a medium bowl, combine the chili powder, oregano, sugar, and salt. Measure out 1 tablespoon of the chili mixture and set aside to use on the steak in step 3. Add the onions to the spice mixture remaining in the bowl, and toss to coat.

2 Place the onions on a broiler pan. Place the peppers, skin-side up, alongside the onions on the pan. Broil 4 to 6 inches from the heat, turning the onions occasionally (do not turn the peppers), until the onions are tender but still slightly crisp and the peppers are charred, about 10 minutes. When cool enough to handle, peel the peppers and thickly slice.

3 Brush the flank steak with the lime juice. Rub the reserved tablespoon chili mixture into the steak. Broil, turning once, for 10 minutes, or until medium-rare. Let stand for 5 minutes before thinly slicing. Meanwhile, place the tortillas under the broiler for 30 seconds to warm through.

4 Serve each person 2 tortillas, grilled steak and vegetables, and yogurt.
Makes 4 servings

F.Y.I.

Flour tortillas are round, thin Mexican flatbreads made of wheat flour, water, and a solid fat—traditionally lard, but American supermarket versions are usually made with vegetable shortening. Flour tortillas come in a wide range of sizes, from 6 inches in diameter up to 10 inches, and sometimes bigger. The larger tortillas are sometimes sold as "burrito-style" tortillas. The downside to flour tortillas is their fat content, but there are low-fat and fat-free versions available.

Honey-Mustard Pork & Sweet Potatoes

Pork tenderloin, in addition to being the leanest cut of pork, is convenient for time-pressured cooks. In this recipe, it roasts in just 30 minutes on a bed of vegetables that are then transformed into a delicious sauce.

1 pound sweet potatoes, peeled and thinly sliced
1 large red bell pepper, cut into ½-inch squares
1 large green bell pepper, cut into ½-inch squares
3 cloves garlic, slivered
¼ teaspoon salt
¼ teaspoon black pepper
⅔ cup chicken broth, homemade (*page 25*) or
   reduced-sodium canned, or Onion Broth (*page 25*)
2 tablespoons honey
1 tablespoon mustard
2 teaspoons fresh lemon juice
1 pound pork tenderloin

1 Preheat the oven to 425°F.

2 In a large bowl, combine the sweet potatoes, bell peppers, garlic, salt, and black pepper, and toss until well combined.

3 Spoon the vegetables into a 7 x 11-inch baking pan and toss with ⅓ cup of the chicken broth. Cover with foil and bake for 15 minutes.

4 Meanwhile, in a small bowl, stir together the honey, mustard, and lemon juice.

5 Pour half the honey-mustard mixture over the vegetables. Place the pork on top of the sweet potato mixture and brush with the remaining honey-mustard mixture. Roast uncovered for 30 minutes, or until the pork is cooked through and the vegetables are tender.

6 Transfer the pork to a cutting board and let stand for 10 minutes before slicing.

7 Meanwhile, spoon 1 cup of the vegetable mixture into a food processor and puree with the remaining ⅓ cup chicken broth. Slice the pork and serve topped with the vegetable puree, with the roasted vegetables on the side. *Makes 4 servings*

Unstuffed Peppers

In a traditional stuffed pepper recipe, rice and often ground beef are packed into a whole bell pepper and braised in tomato sauce. Here, all the components and flavors of stuffed peppers are turned into an easy skillet dish.

per serving	
calories	479
total fat	7.9g
saturated fat	2.8g
cholesterol	46mg
dietary fiber	11g
carbohydrate	70g
protein	35g
sodium	405mg

good source of: beta carotene, fiber, folate, iron, niacin, potassium, thiamin, vitamin B$_{12}$, vitamin B$_6$, vitamin C, zinc

⅔ cup rice
6 ounces well-trimmed beef top round, cut into chunks
1 teaspoon plus 1 tablespoon chili powder
2 teaspoons olive oil
2 cloves garlic, minced
3 large red bell peppers, cut into ¾-inch-wide strips
½ teaspoon oregano
½ teaspoon black pepper
¼ teaspoon salt
1 can (14½ ounces) no-salt-added stewed tomatoes
1 can (8 ounces) no-salt-added tomato sauce
1 can (10½ ounces) kidney beans, rinsed and drained
Several drops of hot pepper sauce (optional)
½ cup shredded reduced-fat sharp Cheddar cheese

1 In a medium saucepan, cook the rice according to package directions, but omit the salt. Remove from the heat and set aside.

2 Meanwhile, place the beef in a food processor and process just until ground. Add 1 teaspoon of the chili powder and pulse just until mixed.

3 In a Dutch oven or flameproof casserole, heat the oil over medium heat. Add the garlic and beef. Cook, stirring, until the beef is lightly browned, 1 to 2 minutes.

4 Stir in the bell peppers, remaining 1 tablespoon chili powder, the oregano, black pepper, and salt. Cook for 2 minutes.

5 Add the stewed tomatoes, tomato sauce, and beans. Increase the heat to high and bring to a boil. Reduce the heat to medium-low, cover, and simmer, stirring occasionally, until the peppers are tender and the flavors have blended, 10 to 15 minutes. Add the hot pepper sauce (if using).

6 Spoon the rice into bowls. Top with the chili and sprinkle with the cheese.
Makes 4 servings

F.Y.I.

One cup of cooked bok choy will give you 24% of the RDA for beta carotene, 17% of the RDA for vitamin B_6, and almost half (49%) of the RDA for vitamin C. Also rich in iron, folate, calcium, fiber, and potassium, bok choy offers an impressive array of nutrients.

Capellini with Barbecued Pork & Vegetables

Dishes that combine a variety of cooked ingredients in broth are common in much of Asia.

> ½ pound well-trimmed boneless pork loin
> 2 tablespoons chili sauce
> 1 tablespoon reduced-sodium soy sauce
> 2 cloves garlic, minced
> 2 teaspoons grated fresh ginger
> 1½ teaspoons dark sesame oil
> 2 cups chicken broth, homemade (*page 25*) or
>   reduced-sodium canned
> ¾ pound bok choy, cut into 1-inch pieces (about 4 cups)
> 2 carrots, thinly sliced on the diagonal
> 3 scallions, sliced
> 6 ounces capellini (angel hair pasta), broken into thirds

1 Cut the pork crosswise into 4 slices.

2 Preheat the broiler. In a small bowl, mix the chili sauce, 1 teaspoon of soy sauce, half the garlic, 1 teaspoon of ginger, and 1 teaspoon of sesame oil. Spread half of the mixture over one side of the pork slices and let stand 10 minutes.

3 Meanwhile, in a large saucepan, combine the broth, remaining 2 teaspoons soy sauce, garlic, and 1 teaspoon ginger. Cover and bring to a boil over high heat. Reduce to low and simmer 5 minutes.

4 Add the bok choy and carrots to the broth. Bring to a boil over high heat, reduce the heat to medium, cover, and simmer until the carrots are tender, 6 to 8 minutes. Stir in the scallions and remove from the heat.

5 Meanwhile, broil the pork 4 to 6 inches from the heat for 3 minutes. Turn the pork over, brush with the remaining chili sauce mixture, and broil for 2 to 3 minutes, or until cooked through but still juicy.

6 In a large pot of boiling water, cook the pasta according to package directions. Drain and toss with the remaining ½ teaspoon sesame oil.

7 Cut the pork crosswise into thin slices. Stir the pasta into the broth, ladle the mixture into bowls, and top with sliced pork. ***Makes 4 servings***

Pot Roast with Winter Vegetables

per serving	
calories	374
total fat	8.2g
saturated fat	2.3g
cholesterol	67mg
dietary fiber	7g
carbohydrate	47g
protein	29g
sodium	445mg

good source of: beta carotene, niacin, potassium, riboflavin, vitamin B$_{12}$, vitamin B$_6$, vitamin C, zinc

Six different vegetables cook with this moist and juicy pot roast. Serve this one-pot dinner with good crusty bread or dinner rolls.

3 cloves garlic, minced
1½ teaspoons rosemary, minced
1½ teaspoons coarsely cracked black pepper
1 teaspoon salt
2 pounds well-trimmed beef rump roast
1½ pounds sweet potatoes, peeled and cut into 1-inch chunks
1½ pounds small red potatoes, cut into ¾-inch wedges
2 large onions, cut into ½-inch wedges
3 large carrots, cut into 1-inch chunks
3 medium parsnips, cut into 1-inch chunks
2 large stalks celery, cut into ½-inch pieces
½ cup chicken broth
1 tablespoon olive oil

1 Preheat the oven to 375°F.

2 In a small bowl or cup, combine the garlic, rosemary, 1 teaspoon of the pepper, and ½ teaspoon of the salt. Rub the mixture over the roast.

3 Place the sweet potatoes, red potatoes, onions, carrots, parsnips, and celery in a large roasting pan. Drizzle with the broth and olive oil. Sprinkle with the remaining ½ teaspoon each pepper and salt. Toss to mix.

4 Place the roast on top of the vegetables and roast 1 hour and 15 minutes, stirring vegetables occasionally, or until the meat is rare to medium-rare (135° to 140°F on a meat thermometer).

5 Transfer the roast to a platter and set aside, loosely covered.

6 Return the vegetables to the oven and continue roasting, turning occasionally, for 15 to 20 minutes, or until lightly browned and tender.

7 Transfer the vegetables and pan juices to a large platter. Carve the meat into thin slices and arrange on the platter. Pour any juices from the cutting board over the meat. *Makes 8 servings*

Currant-Glazed Pork Tenderloin

Serve slices of the pork along with steamed asparagus and wild rice. Since the currant jelly used for the glaze is likely to bake onto the pan, line the baking pan with foil to make clean-up easier.

per serving	
calories	196
total fat	4.2g
saturated fat	1.4g
cholesterol	67mg
dietary fiber	0g
carbohydrate	15g
protein	24g
sodium	346mg

good source of: thiamin, selenium

2 cloves garlic, minced
¾ teaspoon rubbed sage
½ teaspoon rosemary, minced
¼ teaspoon salt
¼ teaspoon pepper
¼ teaspoon sugar
1 bay leaf, crushed
1 pound pork tenderloin
¼ cup red currant jelly

1 Preheat the oven to 425°F. In a small bowl, combine the garlic, sage, rosemary, salt, pepper, sugar, and bay leaf. Rub the garlic-herb mixture into the pork. Place the pork in a small baking pan and roast 5 minutes.

2 Meanwhile, in a small saucepan, melt the jelly over low heat. Brush the jelly over the pork. Reduce the oven temperature to 350°F and roast for 30 minutes, brushing every 10 minutes with the jelly, or until the pork is glistening and cooked through but still juicy (about 160°F on a meat thermometer). ***Makes 4 servings***

Apple-Glazed Pork Tenderloin Replace the rosemary with an equal amount of thyme and omit the sugar. Use apple jelly instead of red currant jelly. For an added treat, serve with sautéed apple slices as a side dish.

KITCHEN *tip*

Pork tenderloins, which tend to weigh about 1 pound, often come shrink-wrapped with one or two to a package. If your market only has the double packages, you can rewrap the unused tenderloin and freeze it. Or, if there is a store butcher, see if you can get a single tenderloin before they get wrapped. Avoid those that come packed in marinade since there's often oil added to the mix.

Orange-Mustard Ham Kebabs

Two well-known culinary partnerships are ham and mustard, and sweet potatoes and orange. Here you have both of those great partnerships, but the flavors and ingredients have been reshuffled in a most inventive way.

1½ pounds sweet potatoes, peeled and cut into 1-inch chunks
½ pound reduced-sodium ham, in one piece, cut into 24 cubes
2 yellow summer squash, cut into ½-inch slices
1 medium onion, cut into 1-inch chunks
3 tablespoons frozen orange juice concentrate, thawed
2 tablespoons honey
2 tablespoons coarse-grained mustard
½ teaspoon black pepper

KITCHEN *tip*

If you use wooden skewers for grilling or broiling, soak them in water before using them so they won't burn. Place them in a pan of water and let them soak for at least 30 minutes before you are ready to grill.

1 Place the sweet potatoes in a medium saucepan and add cold water to cover. Cover and bring to a boil over high heat. Reduce the heat to medium and simmer until sweet potatoes are tender but still firm, about 10 minutes. Drain and set aside to cool slightly.

2 Preheat the broiler. Spray a broiler pan with nonstick cooking spray.

3 Thread the sweet potatoes, ham, yellow squash, and onion onto eight 12-inch skewers in the following order: squash, onion, sweet potato, and ham. Place skewers on the broiler pan.

4 In a small bowl, whisk together the orange juice concentrate, honey, mustard, and black pepper.

5 Brush most of the glaze over both sides of the skewers. Broil 4 to 5 inches from the heat for 6 minutes. Turn the skewers and broil 5 minutes, or until the vegetables are tender.

6 Remove from the broiler, brush with the remaining glaze, and serve 2 skewers per person. ***Makes 4 servings***

Spotlite recipe

Jamaican Jerked Chicken

Jamaican cooks are renowned for a style of barbecuing that begins by rubbing the meat or poultry with a heady mixture of spices. The spices are called jerk spices, and the food that has been seasoned with them is referred to as "jerked." Our version of jerked chicken is probably not as hot as a traditional Jamaican rendition, but if you can tolerate the heat, add some cayenne to the mixture.

3 scallions, minced
3 cloves garlic, minced
2 tablespoons minced fresh ginger
1 tablespoon brown sugar
2 teaspoons allspice
½ teaspoon salt
1 pickled jalapeño pepper, minced
¼ teaspoon black pepper
2 tablespoons fresh lime juice
2 teaspoons olive oil
4 small skinless, boneless chicken breast halves
    (4 ounces each)
Corn Salsa (*page 69, optional*)

1 In a small bowl, stir together the scallions, garlic, ginger, brown sugar, allspice, salt, jalapeño, black pepper, lime juice, and oil.

2 Place the chicken in a small nonaluminum baking pan, rub the jerk spice mixture into both sides of the chicken, and set aside.

3 Preheat the broiler. Place the chicken on a broiler pan and broil 4 to 6 inches from the heat for 4 minutes per side, or until the chicken is cooked through. Serve with the Corn Salsa (if using). ***Makes 4 servings***

PER SERVING 169 calories, 5g total fat (1.1g saturated), 63mg cholesterol, 1g dietary fiber, 7g carbohydrate, 23g protein, 364mg sodium
Good source of: niacin, selenium, vitamin B$_6$

Feta-Topped Baked Chicken & Vegetables

The complementary flavors of tomato and feta cheese are a tangy counterpoint to the sweet potatoes in this satisfying baked chicken dish.

per serving	
calories	332
total fat	8.8g
saturated fat	3.6g
cholesterol	124mg
dietary fiber	4g
carbohydrate	32g
protein	32g
sodium	785mg

good source of: beta carotene, niacin, potassium, riboflavin, selenium, vitamin B$_{12}$, vitamin B$_6$, vitamin C, vitamin E, zinc

2 tablespoons fresh lemon juice
1½ teaspoons oregano
¾ teaspoon pepper
½ teaspoon salt
¼ cup water
1¼ pounds unpeeled sweet potatoes, cut into ¾-inch chunks
1 pound plum tomatoes, cut into ½-inch chunks
8 skinless bone-in chicken thighs (3 ounces each)
⅓ cup crumbled feta cheese (2 ounces)

1 Preheat the oven to 400°F. Spray a 9 x 13-inch baking dish with nonstick cooking spray.

2 In a small bowl or cup, mix the lemon juice, oregano, pepper, salt, and water.

3 Spoon half of the lemon juice mixture into the baking dish. Add the sweet potatoes and tomatoes to the dish and toss to combine. Place the chicken on top of the vegetables and drizzle with the remaining lemon juice mixture.

4 Cover with foil and bake 45 minutes, occasionally spooning pan juices over the chicken and vegetables. Uncover and bake 15 to 20 minutes, or until the chicken is cooked through and the vegetables are tender.

5 Crumble the feta evenly over the chicken and vegetables and bake 3 to 4 minutes longer, or until the cheese is melted. *Makes 4 servings*

Greek-Style Chicken Salad Prepare the baked chicken recipe through step 4 and remove the baking pan from the oven. When the chicken is cool enough to handle, cut the meat off the bone and cut into bite-size pieces. In a serving bowl, whisk together ½ cup fat-free yogurt with the ⅓ cup crumbled feta. Stir in ¼ cup chopped fresh mint. Add the chicken and vegetables and toss to combine.

Chicken-Onion Soup

Onions cooked until golden brown add rich, sweet flavor to this delicious and satisfying chicken soup. Shredded Swiss chard adds flavor and beta carotene.

4 teaspoons olive oil

1 large onion, thinly sliced

4 cloves garlic, minced

½ pound skinless, boneless chicken breast

½ teaspoon oregano

½ teaspoon pepper

¼ teaspoon salt

4 cups chicken broth, homemade (*page 25*) or
   reduced-sodium canned, or Onion Broth (*page 25*)

4 large carrots, sliced

4 ounces spaghetti, broken in thirds

4 cups (loosely packed) 1-inch pieces Swiss chard or
   spinach

1 In a large nonstick skillet, heat 2 teaspoons of the oil over high heat. Add the onion and garlic, then reduce the heat to medium-high, and sauté until the onion is lightly browned, 4 to 5 minutes.

2 Push the onion mixture to one side of the skillet and add the remaining 2 teaspoons oil and the chicken. Sprinkle the chicken with ¼ teaspoon of the oregano, ¼ teaspoon of the pepper, and ⅛ teaspoon of the salt. Cook the chicken until lightly browned, about 2 minutes per side.

3 Add ¼ cup of the broth and stir to loosen any browned bits clinging to the bottom of the pan. Reduce the heat to medium and simmer mixture until the chicken is no longer pink in the center, 3 to 4 minutes. Transfer the chicken and half the onion mixture to a plate and cover loosely to keep warm.

4 Transfer the remaining onion mixture to a large saucepan or Dutch oven and add the remaining 3¾ cups broth, the carrots, spaghetti, and remaining ¼ teaspoon oregano, ¼ teaspoon pepper, and ⅛ teaspoon salt. Cover and bring to a boil over high heat. Reduce the heat to medium-low and simmer 5 minutes.

5 Stir in the Swiss chard, cover, and simmer, stirring frequently, until the vegetables and pasta are tender, 4 to 6 minutes (spinach will cook faster).

6 Ladle the soup into bowls. Cut the reserved chicken on an angle into thin slices and arrange on top of each bowl. Spoon the browned onion mixture over the chicken and serve. *Makes 4 servings*

Recipes for Weight Loss

---

per serving	
calories	286
total fat	6g
saturated fat	0.9g
cholesterol	33mg
dietary fiber	4g
carbohydrate	36g
protein	22g
sodium	738mg

good source of: beta carotene, fiber, niacin, selenium, vitamin B₆, vitamin C

F.Y.I.

One cup of cooked Swiss chard will yield 36% of the RDA for magnesium, 30% of the RDA for beta carotene, and 35% of the RDA for vitamin C. And for a low-fat food, it supplies an unusually high amount of vitamin E—one cup cooked chard gives you 22% of the RDA for this antioxidant vitamin. Moreover, Swiss chard is extremely rich in potassium and fiber.

Honey-Brushed Hens

<table>
<tbody>
<tr><td colspan="2">per serving</td></tr>
<tr><td>calories</td><td>269</td></tr>
<tr><td>total fat</td><td>6.1g</td></tr>
<tr><td>saturated fat</td><td>1.6g</td></tr>
<tr><td>cholesterol</td><td>165mg</td></tr>
<tr><td>dietary fiber</td><td>0g</td></tr>
<tr><td>carbohydrate</td><td>14g</td></tr>
<tr><td>protein</td><td>37g</td></tr>
<tr><td>sodium</td><td>99mg</td></tr>
</tbody>
</table>

good source of: niacin, riboflavin, vitamin B$_6$

Cornish game hens are a convenient way of letting each diner have both breast meat and dark meat in one tidy package. However, you could also make this with bone-in chicken breast halves. In either case, be sure to remove the skin before eating.

2 Cornish game hens (1½ pounds each), split in half
½ teaspoon pepper
1 tablespoon grated lemon zest
½ cup unsweetened pineapple juice
2 tablespoons honey
1 tablespoon dark rum
1 tablespoon grated fresh ginger

ON THE *Menu*

Serve these hens with Citrus Salsa (*page 69*) and couscous. For dessert, have Berry Cheesecake Mousse (*page 131*) and espresso.

1 Season the hens with the pepper.

2 In a bowl, combine the lemon zest, pineapple juice, honey, rum, and ginger. Add the hens and turn to coat with the mixture. Let stand until ready to cook, but for at least 10 minutes.

3 Preheat the oven to 450°F.

4 Place the hens in a single layer in a baking pan and add the marinade. Bake for 25 to 30 minutes, basting with the pan juices, until the hens are cooked through.

5 When the hens are done, transfer to a serving platter and cover loosely to keep warm. Pour the pan juices into a gravy separator to remove the fat, then pour the degreased juices into a gravy boat to pass at the table.

6 Remove the game hen skin before eating. *Makes 4 servings*

Cranberry-Ginger Hens Omit the lemon zest and increase the fresh ginger to 2 tablespoons. Substitute cranberry juice for the pineapple juice, orange allfruit spread for the honey, and soy sauce for the rum.

Roast Turkey Salad with Honeydew & Raspberries

This delightful main-course salad combines honeydew melon with red raspberries, turkey, and watercress in a lemon-apricot dressing scented with sesame oil. If you'd like to "fancy it up" a bit, you could use a melon baller for the honeydew instead of cutting it into cubes.

1 honeydew melon (about 4 pounds), seeded
½ cup apricot all-fruit spread
2 teaspoons grated lemon zest
2 tablespoons fresh lemon juice
2 teaspoons dark sesame oil
¾ pound unsliced roast turkey, cut into ½-inch cubes
4 cups sliced romaine lettuce
4 cups watercress, coarse stems removed
1 pint raspberries

1 Cut the honeydew into wedges. Remove the rind, and cut into 1-inch cubes. Place in a bowl and refrigerate while you make the dressing.

2 In a small bowl, blend the apricot fruit spread with the lemon zest, lemon juice and sesame oil.

3 Place the turkey in a medium bowl. Pour half of the dressing over the turkey and toss to coat well.

4 To assemble the salads, make a bed of romaine and watercress on each of 4 plates. Top with the turkey and melon cubes. Drizzle the remaining dressing over the salads and top with the raspberries. *Makes 4 servings*

Chicken Curry with Wide Noodles

In this comfort food dish with an Asian flair, chicken, sweet potatoes, and carrots in a velvety curry sauce are tossed with noodles.

On the *Menu*

This richly flavored chicken and vegetable curry recipe comes with its own side dish built in. There's no need to serve anything else with it, except perhaps some chutney or hot sauce. For dessert, offer chilled orange slices tossed with shredded fresh basil.

1 tablespoon olive oil
3 cloves garlic, minced
1 tablespoon plus 1½ teaspoons curry powder
¾ pound sweet potatoes, peeled and cut into ½-inch chunks
1 large carrot, thinly sliced
1¼ cups chicken broth, homemade (*page 25*) or reduced-sodium canned
½ pound skinless, boneless chicken breast, cut into ½-inch chunks
¼ teaspoon salt
½ cup frozen peas
8 ounces wide "no-yolk" noodles
⅓ cup plain fat-free yogurt
1 tablespoon flour
1 teaspoon creamy peanut butter
3 tablespoons chopped cilantro

1 In a large nonstick skillet, heat the oil over medium heat. Add the garlic and cook until fragrant, about 1 minute. Stir in the curry powder and cook 1 minute.

2 Add the sweet potatoes, carrot and ¼ cup of the broth, and cook, stirring frequently, until the carrot is almost tender, about 4 minutes.

3 Add the chicken, stirring to coat. Then add the remaining 1 cup broth and the salt. Bring to a boil, reduce to a simmer, cover, and cook until the sweet potatoes and chicken are cooked through, about 5 minutes. Stir in the peas.

4 Meanwhile, in a large pot of boiling water, cook the noodles according to package directions. Drain.

5 In a small bowl, blend the yogurt and flour. Whisk the yogurt mixture into the chicken mixture, then stir in the peanut butter. Toss the pasta and cilantro with the curried chicken mixture. *Makes 4 servings*

Barbecued Chicken Salad

In the summer—or if you live in a barbecue-any-time-of-the-year part of the country—cook the chicken on the outdoor grill. Serve this salad either warm or at room temperature.

½ cup ketchup
3 tablespoons cider vinegar
1 tablespoon dark brown sugar
¾ teaspoon ground coriander
4 cups shredded green cabbage
2 carrots, shredded
6 drops of hot pepper sauce
1 pound skinless, boneless chicken breasts
2 scallions, thinly sliced
2 tablespoons chopped cilantro

1 Preheat the broiler. Line a broiler pan with foil.

2 In a large bowl, combine the ketchup, vinegar, brown sugar, and coriander, and stir to blend. Measure out ¼ cup of ketchup mixture to use as a baste for the chicken in step 3.

3 Add the cabbage, carrots, and hot pepper sauce to the remaining ketchup mixture in the bowl and toss to coat thoroughly.

4 Brush the chicken with the reserved ¼ cup ketchup mixture and broil 4 to 6 inches from the heat for 4 minutes per side, or until the chicken is cooked through.

5 When cool enough to handle, slice the chicken on the diagonal. Place the cabbage mixture on 4 plates, and top with the chicken, scallions, and cilantro. ***Makes 4 servings***

Asian Barbecued Chicken Salad In the barbecue sauce (step 2), reduce the ketchup to ¼ cup, add ¼ cup hoisin sauce, and use rice vinegar instead of cider vinegar. For the salad, use Napa cabbage instead of green cabbage.

Mexican-Style Turkey Burgers

per serving	
calories	296
total fat	9.3g
saturated fat	2.6g
cholesterol	68mg
dietary fiber	1g
carbohydrate	32g
protein	21g
sodium	713mg

If you can't find extra-lean ground turkey breast, buy a chunk of turkey breast and grind your own in a food processor. You can omit the ketchup mixture and top the burgers with storebought salsa.

¼ cup ketchup
1 tablespoon red wine vinegar
1 teaspoon cumin
¾ pound extra-lean ground turkey breast
1 slice firm white sandwich bread, crumbled
¼ cup low-fat (1%) milk
4 scallions, thinly sliced
½ cup chopped cilantro
¼ teaspoon salt
¼ teaspoon pepper
4 hamburger rolls, preferably whole-grain
1 large tomato, thinly sliced

1 In a small bowl, combine the ketchup, vinegar, and ½ teaspoon of the cumin. Set aside.

2 In a large bowl, combine the remaining ½ teaspoon cumin, the turkey, bread, milk, scallions, cilantro, salt, and pepper. Mix well and shape the mixture into 4 patties.

3 Preheat the broiler. Broil the burgers 4 to 6 inches from the heat for 4 minutes per side, or until cooked through.

4 Serve the burgers on the rolls with the ketchup mixture and sliced tomato.
Makes 4 servings

ON THE *Menu*

Serve these Mexican-style burgers with a salad of chopped romaine lettuce and minced cilantro. Dress the salad with a low-fat lemon-pepper vinaigrette. For dessert, serve low-fat coffee frozen yogurt drizzled with a little chocolate syrup.

HOMEMADE
fresh salsas

The word salsa, to most people, conjures up a taste image of something spicy. And, in fact, most salsas do have some spicy component. However, the word simply means sauce and you should feel free to leave out, or modify, the spicy heat in these homemade salsas. Most fresh salsas need to be consumed fairly soon after they are made. This is especially true of the Banana-Kiwi Salsa, because there is an enzyme in kiwi (called actinidin) that will turn the other salsa ingredients mushy if they are left to sit together for too long.

Banana-Kiwi Salsa

3 tablespoons fresh lime juice
2 teaspoons dark brown sugar
¼ teaspoon salt
⅛ teaspoon allspice
⅛ teaspoon cayenne pepper
2 bananas, diced
1 large red bell pepper, diced
2 kiwifruit, peeled and diced

In a large bowl, stir together the lime juice, brown sugar, salt, allspice, and cayenne. Add the bananas, bell pepper, and kiwi, and toss to combine. *Makes 3 cups*

PER ½ CUP: 70 CALORIES, 0.4G TOTAL FAT (0.1G SATURATED), 0MG CHOLESTEROL, 2G DIETARY FIBER, 18G CARBOHYDRATE, 1G PROTEIN, 98MG SODIUM. **GOOD SOURCE OF:** POTASSIUM, VITAMIN B_6, VITAMIN C

Citrus Salsa

2 large pink grapefruits
1 navel orange
2 tablespoons honey
1 tablespoon red wine vinegar
1 tablespoon minced crystallized ginger
2 tablespoons chopped fresh basil

1 Remove the peel and white pith from the grapefruits and orange. Working over a bowl, cut out the sections from between the membranes, letting them drop into the bowl.

2 Squeeze the juice from the membranes of the orange and 1 of the grapefruits into the bowl. Cut the grapefruit and orange sections into bite-size pieces.
3 Stir in the honey, vinegar, crystallized ginger, and basil. *Makes 2 cups*

PER ½ CUP: 92 CALORIES, 0.2G TOTAL FAT (0G SATURATED), 0MG CHOLESTEROL, 2G DIETARY FIBER, 24G CARBOHYDRATE, 1G PROTEIN, 3MG SODIUM. **GOOD SOURCE OF:** VITAMIN C

Corn Salsa

3 tablespoons fresh lime juice
1 tablespoon mint jelly
½ teaspoon salt
¼ teaspoon cayenne pepper
1½ cups frozen corn kernels, thawed and drained
2 plum tomatoes, diced
1 red bell pepper, diced
1 scallion, thinly sliced

In a large bowl, stir together the lime juice, mint jelly, salt, and cayenne. Add the corn, tomatoes, bell pepper, and scallion, and toss well. Chill until serving time. *Makes 3 cups*

PER ½ CUP: 61 CALORIES, 0.5G TOTAL FAT (0.1G SATURATED), 0MG CHOLESTEROL, 2G DIETARY FIBER, 15G CARBOHYDRATE, 2G PROTEIN, 198MG SODIUM. **GOOD SOURCE OF:** VITAMIN C

Onion-Chicken Fajitas

In a traditional fajita, the most prominent ingredient would be the beef. Here we've substituted chicken breast and shifted the emphasis away from the meat and onto the healthful vegetables.

per serving	
calories	427
total fat	6.7g
saturated fat	0.8g
cholesterol	37mg
dietary fiber	8g
carbohydrate	70g
protein	26g
sodium	935mg

good source of: beta carotene, fiber, niacin, vitamin B$_6$, vitamin C

3 red bell peppers, cut lengthwise into flat panels
2½ teaspoons cumin
2½ teaspoons coriander
2 teaspoons sugar
¾ teaspoon salt
3 large red onions, cut into thick rings
2 tablespoons balsamic vinegar
2 teaspoons olive oil
½ pound skinless, boneless chicken breast
8 low-fat flour tortillas (6 inches)
½ cup mild or medium-hot bottled salsa
½ cup plain fat-free yogurt

1 Preheat the broiler. Place the bell pepper pieces, skin-side up, on a broiler pan and broil 4 inches from the heat for 12 minutes or until the skin is blackened. (Leave the broiler on.) When the peppers are cool enough to handle, peel them and cut into thick strips. Transfer to a large bowl.

2 Meanwhile, in another large bowl, stir together the cumin, coriander, 1 teaspoon of the sugar, and ½ teaspoon of the salt. Measure out 2 teaspoons of the mixture to use as a rub for the chicken in step 4.

3 To the mixture remaining in the bowl, add the onions and the remaining 1 teaspoon sugar, and toss well. Place the onions on the broiler pan and broil 7 minutes, turning occasionally, until the onions are lightly browned and tender. Add the onions to the bowl with the peppers and stir in the vinegar, oil, and remaining ¼ teaspoon salt.

4 Rub the reserved 2 teaspoons spice mixture into the chicken. Broil 4 to 6 inches from the heat for 8 minutes, or until cooked through, turning the chicken over after 4 minutes. When cool enough to handle, thinly slice.

5 Each diner gets 2 tortillas to use for wrapping up the grilled chicken, grilled vegetables, salsa, and yogurt. *Makes 4 servings*

Provençal Chicken Stew

Fennel, tomato, and orange are all ingredients typical of Provence, in the south of France.

per serving	
calories	295
total fat	6.5g
saturated fat	1.3g
cholesterol	71mg
dietary fiber	10g
carbohydrate	36g
protein	27g
sodium	739mg

good source of: fiber, folate, niacin, potassium, selenium, vitamin B$_6$, vitamin C, zinc

2 teaspoons olive oil
1 bulb fennel (1 pound), stalks discarded, bulb quartered lengthwise and sliced crosswise
1 medium zucchini (8 ounces), halved lengthwise and cut crosswise into 1-inch chunks
6 cloves garlic, minced
¾ pound skinless, boneless chicken thighs, cut into 1-inch chunks
1 can (14½ ounces) crushed tomatoes
3 strips (3 x ½-inch) orange zest
⅓ cup orange juice
½ teaspoon salt
¼ teaspoon rosemary, minced
1 can (15½ ounces) cannellini beans, rinsed and drained

1 In a nonstick Dutch oven, heat the oil over medium heat. Add the fennel and zucchini, and cook, stirring frequently, until the fennel is tender, about 5 minutes.

2 Add the garlic and cook until tender, about 1 minute. Add the chicken and cook, stirring, until the chicken is no longer pink, about 3 minutes.

3 Stir in the tomatoes, orange zest, orange juice, salt, and rosemary, and bring to a boil. Add the beans, reduce to a simmer, cover, and cook until the chicken is cooked through, about 7 minutes. **_Makes 4 servings_**

F.Y.I.

Although the pale green stalks of the fennel plant resemble celery, there is no mistaking fennel's sweet licoricelike flavor, which distinguishes it from its lookalike. Like celery, though, fennel is filling while also low in calories, making it an ideal food for anyone who is watching their weight. Fennel provides vitamin C, potassium, and small amounts of folate.

Pasta with Hunter-Style Chicken

Dishes with "hunter" in their names (*cacciatore* in Italian, *à la chasseur* in French) almost always have a sauce made with mushrooms, tomatoes, and herbs. This pasta sauce follows the European tradition, but uses a non-European mushroom, Asian shiitakes.

¼ cup dried shiitake mushrooms (¼ ounce)
1 cup boiling water
1 tablespoon olive oil
1 small onion, finely chopped
3 cloves garlic, minced
½ pound button mushrooms, thinly sliced
1½ cups canned crushed tomatoes
¾ teaspoon rosemary, minced
½ teaspoon salt
¼ teaspoon crushed red pepper flakes
½ pound skinless, boneless, chicken thighs, cut into
    ½-inch chunks
10 ounces medium pasta shells
¼ cup grated Parmesan cheese

1 In a small heatproof bowl, combine the dried mushrooms and the boiling water, and let stand for 20 minutes or until softened. Reserving the soaking liquid, scoop out the dried mushrooms and coarsely chop. Strain the soaking liquid through a coffee filter or a paper towel-lined sieve.

2 In a large nonstick skillet, heat the oil over medium heat. Add the onion and garlic, and cook until the onion is golden brown, about 5 minutes. Add the dried and fresh button mushrooms, and cook, stirring frequently, until the fresh mushrooms are tender, about 5 minutes.

3 Add the reserved mushroom soaking liquid, the tomatoes, rosemary, salt, and red pepper flakes. Bring to a boil and add the chicken. Reduce to a simmer and cook, uncovered, for 15 minutes, or until the chicken is tender and the sauce is slightly thickened.

4 In a large pot of boiling water, cook the pasta according to package directions. Drain. Transfer the pasta to a large bowl. Add the sauce and Parmesan, and toss to combine. ***Makes 4 servings***

Sweet & Sour Turkey Stir-Fry

If your market has baby bok choy, use it instead of the full-grown version. Just cut these diminutive vegetables crosswise into thirds.

2 teaspoons olive oil
1 pound turkey cutlets, cut into ½-inch-wide strips
1 tablespoon cornstarch
⅓ cup no-salt-added ketchup
2 tablespoons rice vinegar or cider vinegar
1 tablespoon sugar
1 tablespoon plus 1 teaspoon reduced-sodium soy sauce
1 tablespoon minced fresh ginger
3 cloves garlic, minced
2 large carrots, thinly sliced
3 cups sliced bok choy
¼ pound snow peas, trimmed

1 In a large nonstick skillet, heat the oil over medium heat. Dust the turkey with the cornstarch. Add to the skillet and sauté for 2 minutes. Transfer the turkey to a plate and cover loosely to keep warm.

2 In a small bowl, stir together the ketchup, vinegar, sugar, and soy sauce. Set the ketchup mixture aside.

3 Add the ginger and garlic to the skillet and stir-fry until fragrant, about 30 seconds. Add the carrots, bok choy, and snow peas, and stir-fry until the vegetables are crisp-tender, about 4 minutes.

4 Stir in the ketchup mixture and bring to a boil. Return the turkey (and any juices that have collected on the plate) to the skillet and cook until just heated through. **Makes 4 servings**

per serving	
calories	231
total fat	3.3g
saturated fat	0.6g
cholesterol	70mg
dietary fiber	3g
carbohydrate	19g
protein	31g
sodium	522mg

good source of: beta carotene, niacin, potassium, vitamin B_6, vitamin C

ON THE *Menu*

Instead of the more expected rice, serve this Asian-style stir-fry over broad noodles. For dessert, serve wedges of chilled melon or other seasonal fruit.

ON THE *Menu*

Serve this broiled chicken and sauce over spinach fettuccine, with steamed broccoli as a side dish. Offer fruit sorbet and berries for dessert. Or, if you're feeling ambitious, make the Strawberry Long Cake (*page 125*).

Broiled Chicken with Spicy Lemon-Carrot Sauce

As main courses go, this one is not only easy to prepare, but it's exceptionally low in calories—under 200 per serving.

4 small skinless, boneless chicken breast halves
(4 ounces each)
1½ teaspoons grated lemon zest
1 tablespoon plus 2 teaspoons fresh lemon juice
2 cloves garlic, minced
½ teaspoon thyme
¼ teaspoon salt
¼ teaspoon black pepper
1 cup carrot juice
1 tablespoon cornstarch
Large pinch of cayenne pepper

1 Place the chicken on a plate. Sprinkle with the lemon zest, 1 tablespoon of the lemon juice, the garlic, ¼ teaspoon of the thyme, and ⅛ teaspoon each of the salt and black pepper. Rub the seasonings onto the chicken. Cover loosely and set aside while you preheat the broiler and broiler pan.

2 Broil the chicken 4 to 5 inches from the heat for 5 minutes per side, or until cooked through. Transfer the chicken to a clean plate and cover loosely with foil to keep warm.

3 In a small saucepan, whisk the carrot juice into the cornstarch until smooth. Stir in the cayenne and remaining ¼ teaspoon thyme and ⅛ teaspoon each salt and black pepper.

4 Bring the carrot juice mixture to a boil over medium-high heat, stirring constantly. Cook until the sauce is slightly thickened. Remove from the heat and stir in the remaining 2 teaspoons lemon juice. Stir in any juices that have collected on the plate under the chicken. Serve the sauce with the chicken.
Makes 4 servings

Turkey & Sweet Potato Salad with Honey-Mustard Dressing

Some of the best flavors of Thanksgiving are featured in this any-time-of-year salad. Serve the salad with spiced cider—iced or hot, depending on the weather.

1½ pounds sweet potatoes, unpeeled, cut into
   ½-inch chunks
⅓ cup plain fat-free yogurt
3 tablespoons honey
2 tablespoons light mayonnaise
1 tablespoon balsamic vinegar
2 teaspoons Dijon mustard
¼ teaspoon salt
6 ounces smoked turkey, in one piece, cut into
   ½-inch chunks
3 stalks celery, with leaves, thinly sliced
2 scallions, thinly sliced
¾ cup small seedless red grapes
1 bunch watercress, tough stems removed

1 Place the sweet potatoes in a medium saucepan and add cold water to cover. Bring to a boil, covered, over high heat. Reduce the heat to medium and simmer until tender, 5 to 7 minutes.

2 Meanwhile, in a large bowl, whisk together the yogurt, honey, mayonnaise, vinegar, mustard, and salt until blended. Add the warm sweet potatoes and toss gently to combine.

3 Add the turkey, celery, scallions, and grapes, and toss to mix well. Serve the salad on a bed of watercress. **Makes 4 servings**

Chicken in Shiitake-Tomato Sauce

If you can't find fresh shiitake mushrooms, substitute button or cremini mushrooms. The flavor won't be quite as earthy, but it will still be delicious.

per serving	
calories	329
total fat	7.8g
saturated fat	1.7g
cholesterol	109mg
dietary fiber	2g
carbohydrate	11g
protein	44g
sodium	440mg

good source of: niacin, selenium, vitamin B$_6$

    4 bone-in chicken breast halves (6 ounces each), skinned
    2 tablespoons flour
    1 tablespoon olive oil
    ¾ pound fresh shiitake mushrooms, stems discarded and
        caps thickly sliced
    4 cloves garlic, minced
    ⅔ cup dry red wine
    1¼ cups canned crushed tomatoes
    ½ teaspoon rosemary, minced
    ½ teaspoon salt
    ¼ teaspoon pepper

1 Dredge the chicken in the flour, shaking off the excess.

2 In a large nonstick skillet, heat the oil over medium heat. Add the chicken and cook until golden brown, 3 minutes per side. With a slotted spoon, transfer the chicken to a plate.

3 Add the mushrooms and garlic to the pan and cook, stirring frequently, until the mushrooms are lightly browned, about 5 minutes.

4 Add the wine, increase the heat to high, and cook until the wine is reduced by half, about 3 minutes. Add the tomatoes, rosemary, salt, and pepper, and bring to a boil.

5 Return the chicken to the pan, reduce to a simmer, cover, and cook, turning the chicken occasionally, or until the chicken is cooked through, about 20 minutes. *Makes 4 servings*

Italian Sausage Ragù with Fusilli

If you like spicy food, use hot Italian-style turkey sausage in place of the sweet sausages called for here.

10 ounces spinach fusilli
1 large onion, finely chopped
3 cloves garlic, slivered
1 can (28 ounces) crushed tomatoes
½ cup carrot juice
1½ teaspoons fennel seeds
½ pound Italian-style turkey sausage

1 In a large pot of boiling water, cook the fusilli according to package directions. Drain, reserving ⅓ cup of the pasta cooking water.

2 Meanwhile, spray a large nonstick skillet with nonstick cooking spray. Add the onion and garlic, and cook over low heat, stirring frequently, until the onion is tender, about 7 minutes.

3 Add the tomatoes, carrot juice, and fennel seeds, and bring to a boil. Reduce to a simmer, add the whole links of turkey sausage, cover, and cook until the sausage is cooked through, about 10 minutes.

4 With tongs, remove the sausages from the sauce and when cool enough to handle, thinly slice. Return the sliced sausages to the sauce in the skillet and stir to combine.

5 Transfer the sauce to a large bowl. Add the drained pasta and reserved pasta cooking water and toss to combine. ***Makes 4 servings***

ON THE *Menu*

Although this meal is relatively low in fat, it has a substantial number of calories from the pasta. So don't be tempted to serve bread with this dish. Instead, offer a side salad of shredded spinach in a low-fat lemon dressing. For dessert, serve sliced fresh nectarines sprinkled with a little dark rum.

Chicken, Broccoli & Tomato Stir-Fry

If your supermarket sells already cut-up broccoli florets and chicken strips for stir-fries, you can put this meal together in the time it takes to cook the rice.

1 cup rice
½ teaspoon salt
1½ teaspoons cornstarch
1 cup chicken broth, homemade (*page 25*) or reduced-sodium canned
2 tablespoons reduced-sodium soy sauce
1 tablespoon dry sherry or apple juice
1 tablespoon olive oil
10 ounces skinless, boneless chicken thighs, cut into thin strips
5 cups broccoli florets
2 cups cherry tomatoes

1 In a medium saucepan, cook the rice according to package directions, using ¼ teaspoon of salt.

2 Meanwhile, in a small bowl, combine the remaining ¼ teaspoon salt and the cornstarch. Whisk in ⅔ cup of the broth, the soy sauce, and sherry. Set aside.

3 In a large nonstick skillet or wok, heat the oil over medium-high heat. Add the chicken and cook until no longer pink, about 2 minutes.

4 Add the broccoli, tomatoes, and remaining ⅓ cup broth, and cook, stirring frequently, until the chicken is cooked through, 3 to 5 minutes.

5 Stir the broth mixture to recombine. Add it to the pan and cook, stirring, until the sauce is slightly thickened, about 1 minute. Serve over the rice.
Makes 4 servings

Coq au Vin Blanc

White wine—not the traditional red—lends its inimitable flavor to this homespun, but classic, French dish. If you use chicken breasts for this (instead of an assortment of chicken parts), cut them into smaller serving pieces before cooking.

¼ cup flour
½ teaspoon pepper
¼ teaspoon salt
2 pounds bone-in chicken parts, skinned
2 teaspoons olive oil
3 tablespoons diced Canadian bacon (1 ounce)
2 cloves garlic, minced
¾ teaspoon thyme
2 bay leaves
1 cup chicken broth, homemade (*page 25*) or
    reduced-sodium canned
1 cup dry white wine
3 cups carrot sticks
½ pound small mushrooms
1 cup frozen pearl onions

1 Preheat the oven to 450°F. Spray a 9 x 13-inch baking pan with nonstick cooking spray.

2 On a sheet of wax paper, mix the flour with ¼ teaspoon of the pepper and ⅛ teaspoon of the salt. Dredge the chicken in the seasoned flour, reserving any leftover dredging mixture. Arrange the chicken in a single layer in the baking pan and drizzle with 1 teaspoon of the oil. Bake 15 minutes, turning once or twice, until the chicken is light golden.

3 Meanwhile, in a Dutch oven or flameproof casserole, combine the remaining 1 teaspoon oil with the Canadian bacon, garlic, thyme, and bay leaves. Stir-fry over medium heat just until the mixture is fragrant, 2 to 3 minutes.

4 Stir in the reserved dredging mixture and cook, stirring, until the flour is well incorporated, about 30 seconds. Whisk in the broth, then stir in wine until smooth.

5 Add the chicken (and any juices from the pan), carrots, mushrooms, onions, and remaining ¼ teaspoon pepper and ⅛ teaspoon salt. Cover and bring to a boil over high heat, stirring occasionally. Reduce the heat to medium-low and simmer, stirring occasionally, until the chicken is cooked through and the vegetables are tender, about 30 minutes. *Makes 4 servings*

per serving	
calories	381
total fat	7.9g
saturated fat	1.8g
cholesterol	113mg
dietary fiber	4g
carbohydrate	27g
protein	40g
sodium	523mg

good source of: beta carotene, niacin, potassium, riboflavin, selenium, thiamin, vitamin B_{12}, vitamin B_6, zinc

F.Y.I.

Canadian bacon isn't really bacon at all: It's a lean smoked meat, similar to ham. Since Canadian bacon is precooked, it can be used as is; but for the best flavor, sauté it briefly—just until crisped around the edges. A small amount of Canadian bacon (as little as 1 ounce) adds big flavor to dishes, but with much less fat than regular bacon.

Roast Turkey Breast with Garlic, Lemon & Basil

Since turkey skin has a good deal of fat, you should discard it before serving (or eating) it. Therefore, it's wasteful to season the skin itself, as you might in an ordinary roast turkey recipe. Instead, a seasoning mixture of fresh basil, garlic, and lemon is rubbed into the flesh of the turkey *under* the skin.

¾ cup packed fresh basil leaves
8 cloves garlic, peeled
2 tablespoons olive oil
1½ teaspoons grated lemon zest
3 tablespoons fresh lemon juice
1¼ teaspoons salt
1 bone-in turkey breast (4½ pounds)
1 whole lemon

1 Preheat the oven to 400°F. In a food processor, puree the basil, garlic, oil, lemon zest, lemon juice, and 1 teaspoon of the salt.

2 Carefully lift the skin of the turkey breast without removing it. Rub the basil mixture over the turkey flesh and replace the skin. Rub the inside cavity of the turkey with the remaining ¼ teaspoon salt. With a fork, prick the whole lemon in several places. Place the lemon in the turkey cavity.

3 Place the turkey, breastbone down, on a rack in a roasting pan. Pour ½ cup of water into the bottom of the pan. Roast 1 hour and 15 minutes, basting every 15 minutes with the juices in the bottom of the pan.

4 Turn the turkey breastbone up and roast for 30 minutes, or until a meat thermometer registers 165°F (temperature will rise to 170°F as the turkey stands). Let sit 10 minutes and discard the lemon and turkey skin before carving. *Makes 8 servings*

per serving	
calories	276
total fat	4.8g
saturated fat	0.9g
cholesterol	146mg
dietary fiber	1g
carbohydrate	3g
protein	53g
sodium	456mg

good source of: niacin, selenium, vitamin B_{12}, vitamin B_6, zinc

Spotlite recipe

Sloppy Josés

1 tablespoon olive oil
1 large onion, finely chopped
4 cloves garlic, minced
1 green bell pepper, diced
1½ cups TVP (3 ounces)
4 teaspoons chili powder
1 can (28 ounces) crushed tomatoes
1 can (8 ounces) no-salt-added tomato sauce
½ teaspoon salt
¼ cup chopped cilantro
4 whole-wheat rolls, split and toasted

1 In a large nonstick skillet, heat the oil over medium heat. Add the onion and garlic, and cook, stirring frequently, until the onion is golden brown, about 7 minutes.

2 Add the bell pepper and cook until tender, about 5 minutes.

3 Stir in the TVP, chili powder, crushed tomatoes, tomato sauce, and salt, and bring to a boil. Reduce to a simmer, cover, and cook until the mixture is the thickness of spaghetti sauce, about 10 minutes.

4 Stir in the cilantro and spoon the sauce over the rolls. *Makes 4 servings*

PER SERVING 284 calories, 6.2g total fat (0.9g saturated), 0mg cholesterol, 13g dietary fiber, 48g carbohydrate, 19g protein, 726mg sodium
Good source of: fiber, folate, magnesium, niacin, potassium, selenium, thiamin, vitamin B_6, vitamin C

TVP is a type of textured soy protein that comes in both granular and rehydrated forms. Here we use the granular style, which is available in health-food stores, often in bulk. When rehydrated, TVP absorbs flavors well and has a chewy, meatlike texture. This vegetarian Mexican-style sloppy joe mixture would go equally well spooned over cornbread or tossed with pasta.

per serving	
calories	451
total fat	13g
saturated fat	2.6g
cholesterol	7mg
dietary fiber	8g
carbohydrate	67g
protein	19g
sodium	980mg

good source of: fiber, magnesium, niacin, thiamin, vitamin C, zinc

KITCHEN *tip*

An easy way to cut up sun-dried tomatoes that haven't been reconstituted is with a pair of sharp kitchen scissors instead of a knife.

Brown Rice Pasta with Broccoli & Sun-Dried Tomatoes

Even those who are not on a wheat-free diet will enjoy the flavor of pasta made with brown rice (available in health-food stores). For a peppier pasta, add some red pepper flakes when the broccoli goes into the pan. Broccoli rabe can be substituted for broccoli.

¾ pound broccoli florets
12 ounces brown rice pasta or regular penne pasta
⅓ cup sun-dried tomatoes (not oil-packed), cut into thin strips
2 tablespoons olive oil
3 cloves garlic, minced
¼ cup chopped parsley
1 teaspoon salt
½ teaspoon pepper
⅓ cup grated Parmesan cheese

1 In a vegetable steamer, cook the broccoli florets until crisp-tender, 3 to 5 minutes. When cool enough to handle, coarsely chop.

2 In a large pot of boiling water, cook the pasta according to package directions, adding the sun-dried tomatoes for the last 5 minutes of cooking.. Drain, reserving ½ cup of pasta cooking water.

3 Meanwhile, in a large nonstick skillet, heat the oil over medium heat. Add the garlic and cook until fragrant, about 30 seconds. Add the broccoli and cook, stirring, for 2 minutes. Add the drained pasta and tomatoes, parsley, salt, pepper, and reserved pasta cooking water, and toss to combine. Add the Parmesan and toss to combine. ***Makes 4 servings***

Asian Noodle Salad

Asian noodle salads make especially good summer fare as many of them actually improve in flavor when prepared in advance. This variation, with fresh oranges, is as lovely to look at as it is to eat.

8 ounces capellini (angel hair pasta), broken into thirds
1 tablespoon peanut oil
2 navel oranges
2 tablespoons frozen orange juice concentrate
2 tablespoons reduced-sodium soy sauce
1 tablespoon grated fresh ginger
¼ teaspoon salt
1½ cups shredded carrots
1 large red bell pepper, cut into thin strips
2 tablespoons thinly sliced scallions
2 tablespoons coarsely chopped unsalted, dry-roasted peanuts

1 In a large pot of boiling water, cook the pasta according to package directions. Drain, rinse briefly under cold running water, and drain again. Place the pasta in a serving bowl and toss with ½ teaspoon of the oil.

2 Grate 2 teaspoons of zest from one of the oranges. With a serrated knife, remove the peel and white pith from both oranges. Working over a strainer set over a medium bowl, cut out the orange sections from in between the membranes, letting them drop into the strainer. Squeeze the juice from the membranes into the bowl.

3 To the freshly squeezed orange juice in the bowl, add the remaining 2½ teaspoons peanut oil, the orange zest, orange juice concentrate, soy sauce, ginger, and salt, and whisk with a fork to blend.

4 Pour the dressing over the pasta. Add the carrots, bell pepper, and scallions, and toss to blend. Add the orange sections and toss again. Sprinkle with the peanuts. *Makes 4 servings*

F.Y.I.

Slightly earthy and nutty in flavor, peanut oil contains heart-healthy monounsaturated and polyunsaturated fats. It also has a high smoke point, making it a good stir-frying oil. As with all fats and oils, however, it is a concentrated source of calories, so use it in small amounts.

Veggie Burgers

The beef hamburger is appreciated for many reasons—its nutritional attributes, however, are not among them. Veggie "burgers," on the other hand, rarely have the meatiness many people crave. This meatloaf-style burger, seasoned with mint and scallions, manages to bridge the gap.

per serving	
calories	350
total fat	7.4g
saturated fat	1.7g
cholesterol	0mg
dietary fiber	7g
carbohydrate	60g
protein	13g
sodium	665mg

good source of: beta carotene, folate, niacin, riboflavin, thiamin

1 cup water
¼ teaspoon salt
½ cup bulgur
2 large carrots, shredded
4 ounces firm low-fat silken tofu
1 large egg white
3 tablespoons chopped fresh mint
3 tablespoons minced scallions
¼ teaspoon cayenne pepper
⅓ cup plain dried breadcrumbs
¼ cup plus 2 tablespoons flour
2 tablespoons ketchup
2 teaspoons Dijon mustard
1 tablespoon olive oil
4 hamburger buns, preferably whole-grain
4 romaine lettuce leaves
4 large slices tomato

1 In a medium covered saucepan, bring the water and salt to a boil over medium heat. Add the bulgur and carrots, remove from the heat, cover and let stand until the bulgur has softened and absorbed all the liquid, about 30 minutes. Drain and squeeze dry.

2 In a large bowl, mash the tofu. Stir in the bulgur mixture, egg white, mint, scallions, and cayenne, stirring well. Stir in the breadcrumbs, ¼ cup of the flour, the ketchup, and mustard.

3 Preheat the oven to 400°F. Form the bulgur mixture into 4 patties about 1 inch thick and 4 inches in diameter. Dredge the patties in the remaining 2 tablespoons flour.

4 In a large nonstick skillet, heat the oil over medium heat. Add the patties to the skillet and cook until crusty, about 4 minutes per side. Transfer to a nonstick baking sheet and bake 5 minutes, or until heated through.

5 Serve the burgers on hamburger buns with lettuce and tomato. *Makes 4 servings*

KITCHEN*tip*

If you don't have time to soak dried beans overnight before starting to cook them, you can use the quick-soak method: In a large saucepan, combine the beans with cold water to cover by 2 inches. Bring to a boil and cook for 2 minutes. Remove the saucepan from the heat, cover, and let stand for 1 hour. Drain the beans. Return the beans to the saucepan and cook as directed in step 1.

Pasta with White Beans, Carrots & Tomatoes

Sweet caramelized onions, carrot juice, and spicy cayenne pepper form the base of this luscious pasta sauce. If you prefer, you can substitute a 19-ounce can of cannellini beans for the dried. Rinse and drain the canned beans to get rid of most of the sodium. Reserve ½ cup of the pasta cooking liquid to add to the sauce instead of the bean cooking liquid.

1 cup (8 ounces) dried cannellini beans (white kidney beans)

8 cloves garlic, minced

1 teaspoon grated lemon zest

1 teaspoon dried sage

12 ounces whole-wheat penne

1 tablespoon olive oil

2 pounds Spanish onions, diced

2 carrots, quartered lengthwise and thinly sliced crosswise

2 cups carrot juice

1¼ teaspoons salt

¼ teaspoon cayenne pepper

2 large tomatoes, diced

2 tablespoons pine nuts, toasted

1 Place the beans and cold water to cover in a bowl and refrigerate overnight. Drain. Transfer the beans to a large saucepan, add water to cover by 2 inches and bring to a boil over medium heat. Reduce to a simmer, add half the garlic, the lemon zest, and ½ teaspoon of the sage. Partially cover and cook until the beans are tender, about 45 minutes. Drain, reserving ½ cup of the bean cooking liquid.

2 Meanwhile, in a large pot of boiling water, cook the pasta according to package directions. Drain.

3 In a large nonstick skillet, heat the oil over low heat. Add the onions and remaining garlic, and cook, stirring frequently, until the onions are golden brown, about 20 minutes. Add the carrots and cook 5 minutes.

4 Add the carrot juice, salt, cayenne, and remaining ½ teaspoon sage, and bring to a boil. Reduce to a simmer and cook for 10 minutes.

5 Add the cooked beans and reserved bean cooking liquid, and cook 5 minutes. Remove from the heat and transfer to a large bowl. Add the pasta, tomatoes, and pine nuts, and toss to combine. ***Makes 6 servings***

Recipes for Weight Loss

Louisiana Rice & Bean Salad

Wonderful picnic fare, this protein-rich rice dish is a welcome change from potato or macaroni salad. You can make the salad ahead of time and serve it chilled or at room temperature. Adjust the amounts of chilies, chili powder, and hot pepper sauce to taste as this version is not particularly spicy.

per serving	
calories	350
total fat	5.6g
saturated fat	1g
cholesterol	0mg
dietary fiber	11g
carbohydrate	65g
protein	12g
sodium	751mg

good source of: fiber, folate, potassium, selenium, thiamin, vitamin B$_6$, vitamin C

1 can (4 ounces) chopped mild green chilies, drained
¼ cup spicy tomato-vegetable juice
2 tablespoons extra-virgin olive oil
1 tablespoon cider vinegar
1½ teaspoons chili powder
½ to ¾ teaspoon hot pepper sauce
¼ teaspoon salt
3 cups cold cooked rice
2 cans (16 ounces each) pinto beans, rinsed and drained
1 red bell pepper, cut into thin strips
1 green bell pepper, cut into thin strips
1 cup thinly sliced celery
½ cup thinly sliced scallions
Half an avocado, cut into ⅓-inch chunks

1 In a large bowl, stir together the chilies, tomato-vegetable juice, oil, vinegar, chili powder, hot pepper sauce, and salt.

2 Add the rice, beans, bell peppers, celery, and scallions to the dressing and toss to mix. Serve the salad topped with avocado. *Makes 4 servings*

Red Bean, Rice & Shrimp Salad Decrease the beans to 1 can. Omit the avocado. Add ¾ pound cooked medium shrimp.

KITCHEN *tip*

Here's a trick to use if you don't have canned green chilies on hand. Dice a green bell pepper and microwave it, loosely covered, with a squeeze of lemon juice and a dash of hot pepper sauce. Cook just until the pepper is softened. Start out with 45 seconds on high power and then check it. Continue in small increments of time until the pepper is soft.

Szechuan Stir-Fried Vegetables

Serve this vegetable stir-fry fry with rice. Try jasmine rice—a variety frequently used in Thai and other Asian cuisines—for its wonderfully delicate fragrance and firm texture.

¼ cup hoisin sauce
2 tablespoons dry sherry
2 tablespoons honey
¼ teaspoon crushed red pepper flakes
½ cup water
2 teaspoons dark sesame oil
⅓ cup sliced scallions
3 cloves garlic, minced
1 tablespoon minced fresh ginger
1 large red bell pepper, diced
2 large carrots, shredded
6 ounces snow peas, sliced on the diagonal
1 cup canned baby corn, rinsed and drained
1 can (8 ounces) sliced water chestnuts, drained
1 pound extra-firm low-fat silken tofu, cut into 1-inch cubes
2 teaspoons cornstarch blended with 1 tablespoon water

1 In a small bowl, stir together the hoisin sauce, sherry, honey, red pepper flakes, and water. Set aside.

2 In a large nonstick skillet, heat the sesame oil over medium heat. Add the scallions, garlic, and ginger, and cook until softened, about 2 minutes. Stir in the bell pepper and carrots, and sauté until the vegetables are crisp-tender, about 2 minutes.

3 Add the snow peas, baby corn, and water chestnuts, and cook, stirring frequently, until the snow peas are crisp-tender, about 2 minutes.

4 Add the hoisin mixture and tofu, bring to a boil, and cook until the tofu is hot, about 1 minute. Stir in the cornstarch mixture, bring to a boil, and boil until sauce is slightly thickened, about 1 minute. ***Makes 4 servings***

F.Y.I.

Hoisin sauce is a thick, slightly sweet sauce (made from soybeans, chilies, garlic, and spices) used in Chinese cooking. Once opened, it will keep in the refrigerator for several months. If you can't find hoisin sauce, you can make a reasonable alternative with prune butter, which is widely available in supermarkets. For 1 cup of "hoisin" sauce, combine: 1 cup prune butter, 1 tablespoon white vinegar, 2 cloves minced garlic, and ½ teaspoon each crushed red pepper flakes, salt, and cinnamon.

per serving	
calories	278
total fat	5.1g
saturated fat	1.1g
cholesterol	4mg
dietary fiber	5g
carbohydrate	49g
protein	12g
sodium	694mg

good source of: niacin, thiamin, vitamin C

Fettuccine & Sugar Snaps with Almond-Orange Pesto

Although the best known pesto is the basil-based sauce from Genoa, the basic concept (pesto simply means "paste" in Italian) can be used for any number of sauces, such as this parsley-based pesto made with almonds and orange juice.

1 cup packed flat-leaf parsley sprigs
2 tablespoons frozen orange juice concentrate
3 tablespoons grated Parmesan cheese
2 tablespoons slivered almonds, toasted
1 clove garlic, peeled
¾ teaspoon salt
½ teaspoon black pepper
½ pound sugar snap peas, strings removed
2 large yellow bell peppers, thinly sliced
8 ounces fettuccine

1 In a food processor, combine the parsley, orange juice concentrate, Parmesan, almonds, garlic, salt, and black pepper. Process until pureed. Place the pesto in a large serving bowl and set aside.

2 In a vegetable steamer, cook the sugar snaps and bell peppers until the sugar snaps are tender, about 3 minutes.

3 Meanwhile, in a large pot of boiling water, cook the pasta according to package directions. Drain, reserving ¼ cup of the pasta cooking liquid.

4 Stir the pasta cooking liquid into the pesto. Add the drained pasta and vegetables (with their liquid) and toss to coat well. *Makes 4 servings*

Off-the-Shelf

This delicious vegetarian
pizza can be pulled
together in about 25 min-
utes, and most of that time
is unattended cooking
when the pizza is in the
oven. If you can't find
jarred giardiniera (Italian
pickled vegetables) in the
pickle section of the supermarket, you could scatter
chopped tomatoes over the
top of the bean mixture.

Chick-Pea & Pesto Pizza

1 can (15½ ounces) chick-peas, rinsed and drained
¼ cup no-salt-added ketchup
2 tablespoons storebought pesto
¼ cup water
1 large (12 inches) prebaked thin pizza crust
1 cup giardiniera (pickled vegetables), rinsed, drained,
    and finely chopped

1 Preheat the oven to 450°F.

2 In a food processor, combine the chick-peas, ketchup, pesto, and water, and puree until smooth.

3 Place the pizza crust on a large baking sheet. Spread the chick-pea mixture over the crust.

4 Scatter the giardiniera over the chick-pea mixture and bake until the crust is crisp and the topping is piping hot, about 15 minutes. *Makes 4 servings*

PER SERVING **369 calories, 9.6g total fat (2.3g saturated), 2mg cholesterol, 7g dietary fiber, 55g carbohydrate, 15g protein, 893mg sodium**
Good source of: **folate**

Penne with Ratatouille Sauce

The famous vegetable stew of Provence, ratatouille, redolent of fresh herbs and plenty of garlic, serves as an ideal topping for pasta. Pretty here over penne pasta, this ratatouille sauce can also be layered with cooked lasagna noodles, sprinkled with cheese, and baked.

<table>
<tr><th colspan="2">per serving</th></tr>
<tr><td>calories</td><td>410</td></tr>
<tr><td>total fat</td><td>5.4g</td></tr>
<tr><td>saturated fat</td><td>0.8g</td></tr>
<tr><td>cholesterol</td><td>0mg</td></tr>
<tr><td>dietary fiber</td><td>9g</td></tr>
<tr><td>carbohydrate</td><td>79g</td></tr>
<tr><td>protein</td><td>14g</td></tr>
<tr><td>sodium</td><td>376mg</td></tr>
</table>

good source of: fiber, folate, niacin, potassium, riboflavin, selenium, thiamin, vitamin B$_6$, vitamin C, vitamin E

1 tablespoon olive oil
2 small Japanese eggplants, cut crosswise into ½-inch slices
1 large green bell pepper, diced
2 medium zucchini, cut into ½-inch chunks
1 large onion, coarsely chopped
5 cloves garlic, minced
¾ cup chopped fresh basil
1 can (35 ounces) whole tomatoes, chopped with their juice
¾ teaspoon black pepper
¼ teaspoon crushed red pepper flakes
12 ounces penne or other tube-shaped pasta

1 In a large nonstick skillet, heat the oil over medium heat. Stir in the eggplant, bell pepper, zucchini, onion, and garlic. Stir-fry until the vegetables begin to soften, about 10 minutes. Stir in ¼ cup of the basil. Reduce the heat to medium-low, cover and cook until vegetables are very tender, about 10 minutes.

2 Add the tomatoes, black pepper, and red pepper flakes. Bring to a boil over medium-high heat. Reduce the heat to low and simmer while you cook the pasta.

3 In a large pot of boiling water, cook the pasta according to package directions. Drain the pasta and transfer to individual dinner plates.

4 Spoon the sauce over the penne. Sprinkle with the remaining ½ cup basil.
Makes 4 servings

F.Y.I.

High in fiber and low in fat, eggplant has a full flavor and a substantial, "meaty" texture that makes it an ideal food for vegetarians.

Spinach, Tomato & Pasta Salad

The green of the spinach and peas, and the red of the tomatoes, would look very festive with tricolor fusilli or radiatore pasta.

3 tablespoons red wine vinegar
2 tablespoons honey
2 tablespoons Dijon mustard
2 tablespoons light mayonnaise
1½ teaspoons oregano
1 clove garlic, minced
6 ounces fusilli pasta
3 cups loosely packed torn spinach leaves
2 cups diced tomatoes
1 package (10 ounces) frozen peas, thawed
1 tablespoon chopped almonds, toasted

1 In a large bowl, combine the vinegar, honey, mustard, mayonnaise, oregano and garlic, and whisk to blend.

2 In a large pot of boiling water cook the pasta according to package directions. Drain. Add the pasta to the bowl with the dressing. Toss to combine.

3 Add the spinach, tomatoes, peas, and almonds, and toss well. *Makes 4 servings*

Spinach & Sesame Pasta Salad In the dressing, use white wine vinegar instead of red wine vinegar, and stir in ½ teaspoon of dark sesame oil. Substitute 1 teaspoon of ground cumin for the oregano. Sprinkle the salad with 2 teaspoons toasted sesame seeds instead of almonds.

Winter Vegetable Couscous

Parsnips, vastly underrated vegetables, have a sturdy texture and a slightly sweet flavor. However, if your market doesn't carry parsnips, use more carrots.

per serving	
calories	410
total fat	6g
saturated fat	0.8g
cholesterol	0mg
dietary fiber	13g
carbohydrate	77g
protein	14g
sodium	673mg

good source of: beta carotene, fiber, folate, potassium, thiamin, vitamin B₆, vitamin C, vitamin E

1 tablespoon olive oil
2 carrots, thinly sliced
2 parsnips, peeled and thinly sliced
1 red bell pepper, cut into ½-inch chunks
2 teaspoons paprika
1½ teaspoons curry powder
¾ teaspoon salt
¼ teaspoon black pepper
1 can (15½ ounces) chick-peas, rinsed and drained
½ cup carrot juice or tomato-vegetable juice
1 cup couscous
¼ cup plain fat-free yogurt

1 In a large nonstick skillet, heat the oil over medium heat. Add the carrots, parsnips, and bell pepper, and cook until the carrots are crisp-tender, about 5 minutes.

2 Add the paprika, curry powder, ½ teaspoon of the salt, and the black pepper, and stir until the vegetables are well coated. Add the chick-peas and carrot juice, and cook until the chick-peas are heated through, about 3 minutes.

3 Meanwhile, in a medium saucepan, cook the couscous according to package directions, using the remaining ¼ teaspoon salt. Fluff the couscous with a fork and divide among 4 plates. Top with the vegetable mixture and a dollop of the yogurt. ***Makes 4 servings***

Rutabaga & Black Bean Couscous Use 3 cups diced rutabaga instead of the carrots and parsnips. Substitute one 15½-ounce can of black beans, rinsed and drained, for the chick-peas.

Shiitake Marinara Sauce

This hearty mushroom-tomato sauce makes enough to for 1½ pounds of pasta, which should serve about 8 people. If you do not have enough hungry people to feed at one sitting, freeze the sauce in 1- or 2-cup containers.

½ cup dried shiitake mushrooms (½ ounce)
1 cup boiling water
1 tablespoon olive oil
1 large onion, finely chopped
4 cloves garlic, slivered
1 pound fresh shiitake mushrooms, stems discarded and
    caps thinly sliced
½ pound button mushrooms, thinly sliced
1 can (35 ounces) whole tomatoes
1 can (28 ounces) crushed tomatoes
1¼ teaspoons salt
¾ teaspoon pepper
¾ teaspoon cumin

1 In a small heatproof bowl, combine the dried mushrooms and the boiling water, and let stand for 20 minutes or until softened. Reserving the soaking liquid, scoop out the dried mushrooms and coarsely chop. Strain the soaking liquid through a coffee filter or a paper towel-lined sieve.

2 In a large nonstick skillet, heat the olive oil over low heat. Add the onion and garlic, and cook, stirring frequently, until the onion is tender, about 7 minutes.

3 Add the dried mushrooms, fresh shiitake, and fresh button mushrooms, and cook, stirring frequently, until the mushrooms are tender, 7 to 10 minutes. Add the reserved mushroom soaking liquid and bring to a boil. Boil 4 minutes or until almost all the liquid has been absorbed.

4 Add the whole tomatoes, crushed tomatoes, salt, pepper, and cumin, and bring to a boil. With a wooden spoon, break up the whole tomatoes. Reduce to a simmer and cook, uncovered, until the sauce is flavorful and slightly thickened, about 15 minutes. ***Makes 8 servings***

KITCHEN *tip*

Dried shiitake mushrooms can come sliced or as whole caps. If you have whole caps, discard the inedible stems before chopping the mushrooms. Sometimes, if the stem is long enough, you can break it off the cap before softening the mushrooms in boiling water.

Portobello Cheeseburgers

Portobello mushrooms (which are overgrown cremini mushrooms) grow to a size that make them a perfect fit for a hamburger bun. Each cheese in the topping contributes something different: The fat-free mozzarella provides heft, and feta cheese provides intense flavor (which is why such a small amount is needed).

per serving	
calories	262
total fat	4g
saturated fat	1.6g
cholesterol	11mg
dietary fiber	9g
carbohydrate	37g
protein	24g
sodium	872mg

good source of: calcium, fiber, selenium

4 portobello mushrooms (4 ounces each), stems removed
3 tablespoons balsamic vinegar
1 tablespoon reduced-sodium soy sauce
6 ounces shredded fat-free mozzarella
2 tablespoons crumbled feta cheese (1 ounce)
4 whole-wheat rolls, split and toasted
3 cups mixed baby greens

1 Preheat the oven to 450°F. With a spoon or paring knife, scrape out the black gills from the underside of the mushrooms and discard.

2 In a shallow pan large enough to hold the mushrooms snugly in a single layer, stir together the vinegar and soy sauce. Add the mushroom caps and turn them over several times to coat them well with the vinegar mixture. Arrange the mushrooms stemmed-side up and let stand 5 minutes so that they absorb most of the liquid.

3 Bake the mushrooms, turning them over once, until tender, about 10 minutes. Turn the mushrooms stemmed-side up again and top with the mozzarella and feta cheese. Bake until the cheese has melted, about 3 minutes.

4 Top the toasted rolls with the greens and mushrooms. *Makes 4 servings*

KITCHEN *tip*

Scraping the gills (the dark feathery undersides) off the portobello mushrooms keeps them from releasing as much liquid when they cook.

Grilled Vegetable Salad

Grilled asparagus are delicious, but the long, skinny stalks are impossible to grill unless you have either a grill topper or a grilling basket of some sort. If you don't, broil the vegetables instead of grilling.

2 tablespoons water
1 teaspoon plus 1 tablespoon olive oil
½ pound asparagus
2 red bell peppers, cut lengthwise into flat panels
⅓ cup balsamic vinegar
⅓ cup orange juice
1 tablespoon Dijon mustard
2 teaspoons light brown sugar
½ teaspoon ground ginger
¼ teaspoon salt
8 ounces linguine
8 ounces extra-firm low-fat silken tofu, cut into ½-inch chunks

1 Spray a grill topper with nonstick cooking spray. Preheat the grill. In a shallow bowl, whisk together the water and 1 teaspoon of the oil. Add the asparagus, tossing to coat.

2 Place the asparagus on the grill topper. Place the pepper panels, skin-side down, on the grill topper. Grill until the pepper skins are charred and the asparagus are golden brown, about 7 minutes. Turn the asparagus as they color. When cool enough to handle, peel the peppers and cut into ½-inch-wide strips. Cut the asparagus into 1-inch lengths.

3 Meanwhile, in a large bowl, whisk together the remaining 1 tablespoon oil, the vinegar, orange juice, mustard, brown sugar, ginger, and salt.

4 In a large pot of boiling water, cook the pasta according to package directions. Drain and add to the bowl of dressing.

5 Add the asparagus, bell pepper, and tofu to the bowl, and toss to combine. Serve at room temperature or chilled. *Makes 4 servings*

Bean & Butternut Chili

Black beans and chick-peas are two of the more characterful members of the legume world. Chick-peas have a sturdy, meaty texture and black beans have an earthy, smoky flavor—two bonuses in a meatless dish.

per serving	
calories	248
total fat	3.4g
saturated fat	0.5g
cholesterol	0mg
dietary fiber	11g
carbohydrate	46g
protein	12g
sodium	663mg

good source of:
beta carotene, fiber, folate, potassium, thiamin, vitamin C

1 tablespoon olive oil
1 large onion, finely chopped
4 cloves garlic, minced
2 red bell peppers, diced
2 cups butternut squash chunks (1-inch)
1 tablespoon chili powder
¾ teaspoon ground ginger
½ teaspoon salt
1 can (14½ ounces) stewed tomatoes
1 can (6 ounces) tomato paste
1 cup water
2 cans (19 ounces each) black beans, rinsed and drained
1 can (19 ounces) chick-peas, rinsed and drained

1 In a nonstick Dutch oven, heat the oil over medium heat. Add the onion and garlic, and cook, stirring frequently, until the onion is tender, about 10 minutes.

2 Add the bell peppers and squash, stirring to coat. Stir in the chili powder, ginger, and salt. Reduce the heat to medium-low. Cover and cook until the squash is crisp-tender, about 10 minutes.

3 Stir in the stewed tomatoes, tomato paste, and water, and bring to a boil. Reduce to a simmer, cover, and cook until the mixture is slightly thickened, about 5 minutes.

4 Stir in the black beans and chick-peas, and cook, uncovered, until the flavors have blended, the squash is tender, and the beans are heated through, about 5 minutes. *Makes 8 servings*

KITCHEN tip

Butternut squash can be quite difficult to cut, especially the larger specimens. But there is a way to make it a bit easier. First, be sure you have a big, sturdy knife. Then, cut the squash crosswise at the "waist"—the point where the squash starts to bulge out. Place the bulbous end on the work surface cut-side down and cut it in half lengthwise. Now you can scoop out the seeds. Cut the narrower end of the squash in half lengthwise, and peel the 4 pieces of squash. Then cut the squash as directed in the recipe.

Spotlite recipe

Polenta with Meatless Mushroom Sauce

½ cup dried shiitake mushrooms (½ ounce)
1 cup boiling water
1 tablespoon olive oil
1 small onion, finely chopped
2 cloves garlic, minced
½ pound fresh shiitake mushrooms, stems discarded and caps thinly sliced
1¼ cups TVP (2¼ ounces)
1 can (28 ounces) crushed tomatoes
1 teaspoon salt
¾ teaspoon dried rosemary, minced
1 cup yellow cornmeal
3⅔ cups cold water

Polenta, a staple of northern Italian meals for centuries, is nothing more than cornmeal mush. Bland and soothing, polenta can be sauced in many ways. In this meatless polenta recipe, the hearty sauce is made with full-flavored dried and fresh shiitake mushrooms; TVP (textured vegetable protein) provides a meaty texture.

1 In a medium heatproof bowl, soak the dried mushrooms in the boiling water for 20 minutes. Reserving the soaking liquid, scoop out the mushrooms and chop. Strain the liquid through a coffee filter.

2 In a large nonstick skillet, heat the oil over medium heat. Add the onion and garlic, and cook, stirring, until tender, about 7 minutes. Add the dried and fresh mushrooms, and cook until tender, 3 to 4 minutes.

3 Stir in the TVP and the mushroom liquid and bring to a boil. Add the tomatoes, ½ teaspoon of salt, and rosemary; bring to a boil. Reduce to a simmer and cook until thickened, about 7 minutes. Remove from the heat.

4 In a medium bowl, combine the cornmeal and 1 cup of cold water. In a medium saucepan, bring the remaining 2⅔ cups water and remaining ½ teaspoon salt to a boil over high heat. Reduce to a simmer and stir in the cornmeal. Cook, stirring, until the polenta is thick but spoonable, about 5 minutes. Serve the polenta topped with the sauce. *Makes 4 servings*

PER SERVING **357 calories, 5.3g total fat (0.7g saturated), 0mg cholesterol, 13g dietary fiber, 64g carbohydrate, 20g protein, 864mg sodium**
Good source of: **fiber, folate, niacin, potassium, selenium, thiamin, vitamin B$_{12}$, vitamin B$_6$, vitamin D, zinc**

Cremini, Broccoli & Corn Salad

Cremini mushrooms are compact, brown-skinned mushrooms that, except for their color, resemble regular button mushrooms. When cremini mushrooms are allowed to grow until they are quite large (4 inches across or larger), they are marketed as portobello mushrooms.

per serving	
calories	159
total fat	4.7g
saturated fat	0.7g
cholesterol	0mg
dietary fiber	6g
carbohydrate	23g
protein	11g
sodium	692mg

good source of:
vitamin C

3 tablespoons rice vinegar
2 tablespoons fresh lime juice
3 tablespoons reduced-sodium soy sauce
1 tablespoon dark sesame oil
2 teaspoons Dijon mustard
2 teaspoons dark brown sugar
¼ teaspoon salt
½ cup water
¾ pound cremini mushrooms, thinly sliced
3 cups small broccoli florets
1 cup frozen corn kernels, thawed
1 red bell pepper, cut into ¼-inch-wide strips
8 ounces extra-firm low-fat silken tofu, cut into ½-inch cubes

1 In a large bowl, whisk together the vinegar, lime juice, soy sauce, oil, mustard, brown sugar, and salt until well combined.

2 In a large nonstick skillet, heat the water over medium heat. Add the mushrooms and cook, stirring occasionally, until the mushrooms are firm-tender, about 3 minutes. Add the broccoli and cook until crisp-tender, about 3 minutes. Stir in the corn and cook until the corn is heated through, about 2 minutes.

3 Transfer the mixture, along with any liquid remaining in the pan, to the bowl with the dressing. Add the bell pepper and tofu, and toss gently to combine. Serve at room temperature or chilled. ***Makes 4 servings***

KITCHEN *tip*

The reason for seeding a cucumber is to remove the excess liquid that surrounds the seeds, which can make salads soggy. To seed a cucumber, halve it lengthwise. Then take a small spoon (any metal spoon with do, though a grapefruit spoon is especially efficient) and use the tip to scrape out the channel of seeds that runs down the center of the cucumber. This will leave you with a cucumber half that looks like a "U" in cross-section.

Italian Bread Salad with Mozzarella & Roasted Peppers

Using soy mozzarella makes this salad completely dairy-free. However, if you'd prefer, you can use regular mozzarella instead.

2 whole-wheat rolls, preferably sourdough, split
2 cloves garlic, peeled and halved
4 red bell peppers, cut lengthwise into flat panels
3 tablespoons balsamic vinegar
1 tablespoon olive oil
¾ teaspoon salt
1 pint cherry tomatoes, halved
2 cucumbers, peeled, halved lengthwise, seeded, and cut into ½-inch chunks
4 ounces soy mozzarella, cut into ½-inch cubes
3 tablespoons chopped fresh basil

1 Preheat the broiler. Broil the rolls, cut-side up, 6 inches from the heat until golden brown, about 30 seconds. Rub the cut sides of the bread with the garlic. Discard the garlic. When cool enough to handle, cut the bread into 1-inch cubes.

2 Place the bell pepper panels, skin-side up, on the broiler rack. Broil the peppers 4 inches from the heat until charred, about 10 minutes. When cool enough to handle, peel the peppers and cut them into ½-inch-wide strips.

3 Meanwhile, in a large bowl, whisk together the vinegar, oil, and salt. Add the bread cubes, roasted peppers, tomatoes, cucumbers, mozzarella, and basil, and toss well. Let stand at least 30 minutes before serving. Serve the salad at room temperature or chilled. *Makes 4 servings*

Tomato-Orange Braised Leeks

Sweet and spicy, these are great as part of a buffet or vegetable platter.

4 medium leeks
1 cup spicy tomato-vegetable juice
3 strips (3 x ½-inch) orange zest
⅔ cup orange juice
2 cloves garlic, minced
½ teaspoon salt
½ teaspoon thyme
¼ teaspoon cayenne pepper
1 tablespoon olive oil

per serving	
calories	118
total fat	3.8g
saturated fat	0.5g
cholesterol	0mg
dietary fiber	2g
carbohydrate	20g
protein	2g
sodium	504mg

good source of: folate, vitamin B₆, vitamin C

1 Trim the root ends off each leek. Trim off the tough dark green tops, then quarter each leek lengthwise up to but not through the root. Swish the leeks in a bowl of lukewarm water, easing the leaves apart to remove the grit. Lift out the leeks, leaving the grit behind. Repeat as needed with clean water until no grit remains.

2 In a large skillet, combine the spicy tomato-vegetable juice, strips of orange zest, orange juice, garlic, salt, thyme, and cayenne. Bring to a boil, reduce to a simmer, and add the leeks. Cover and cook until the leeks are tender, about 30 minutes.

3 With a slotted spoon, transfer the leeks to a serving platter. Add the oil to the sauce in skillet, return to a boil, and cook, stirring constantly, for 1 minute. Spoon sauce over leeks and serve hot, warm, or chilled. ***Makes 4 servings***

F.Y.I.

The deep orange flesh of butternut squash indicates the presence of carotenoids. In fact, 1 cup of cooked, mashed butternut squash provides 93% of the RDA for the carotenoid, beta carotene. Rich in complex carbohydrates, butternut squash is also a good source of dietary fiber, vitamin C, magnesium, and potassium.

Baked Butternut Squash

Very little is asked of the cook in this recipe, but the rewards, both gustatory and nutritional, are superb. Just note the minuscule amount of fat.

> 2 small butternut squash (1¼ pounds each), halved lengthwise and seeded
> ⅓ cup orange juice
> 2 tablespoons apricot fruit spread
> 2 cloves garlic, minced
> 3 tablespoons chopped parsley
> 1 teaspoon olive oil
> ½ teaspoon salt
> ¼ teaspoon pepper

1 Preheat the oven to 425°F. Cut a small piece off the rounded side of each squash half so that it will sit flat in the pan.

2 In a small bowl, stir together the orange juice, apricot fruit spread, garlic, parsley, oil, salt, and pepper. Spoon the mixture into the hollow of each squash half. Cover with foil and bake until tender, about 45 minutes. ***Makes 4 servings***

Rice-Stuffed Butternut Squash In step 2, omit the orange juice. Combine the remaining ingredients and stir in 1 cup of cooked brown rice. Mound the brown rice in the hollows of the squash, cover, and bake as directed.

Spinach with Garlic & Raisins

Just a hint of sweetness from the raisins (and a touch of sugar) brings out the flavors in this garlic and spinach sauté.

½ cup raisins
1 cup boiling water
2 teaspoons olive oil
4 cloves garlic, minced
2 pounds fresh spinach leaves
½ teaspoon salt
¼ teaspoon sugar
½ teaspoon Louisiana-style hot sauce

1 In a small heatproof bowl, combine the raisins and boiling water and let stand until the raisins are plump and soft, about 10 minutes. Drain, reserving ½ cup of the soaking liquid.

2 Meanwhile, in a nonstick Dutch oven, heat the oil over medium heat. Add the garlic and cook, stirring frequently, until tender, about 1 minute.

3 Add the spinach, salt, and sugar, and stir to coat. Add the raisins, the reserved soaking liquid, and the hot sauce, and cook, stirring frequently, until the spinach is wilted and tender, about 5 minutes. *Makes 4 servings*

F.Y.I.

Vitamin K plays an important role in blood clotting as well as the formation of bone tissue. In addition, vitamin K helps to prevent excessive bleeding; in fact, without vitamin K our blood wouldn't clot properly. Because of its role in blood clotting, people who are on blood-thinning medications should not take vitamin K supplements. In addition to spinach, other foods that are rich in vitamin K include soybeans, cabbage, cauliflower, Swiss chard and other green leafy vegetables.

Chili Corn Pudding

Canned creamed corn helps give this dish its creamy texture. Although the word "cream" is in its name, there is no cream in this velvety type of corn.

F.Y.I.

Lutein is a pigment in the carotenoid family that is being studied for its apparent protective effect against eye conditions such as macular degeneration. Corn, spinach, kale, and egg yolks are lutein-rich foods.

3 tablespoons nonfat dry milk powder
2 tablespoons flour
1 cup fat-free milk
1 pickled jalapeño pepper, minced
2½ teaspoons chili powder
2 teaspoons sugar
¾ teaspoon salt
2 large egg whites
1 package (10 ounces) frozen corn kernels, thawed
1 can (8 ounces) creamed corn
⅓ cup chopped cilantro

1 Preheat the oven to 400°F. Spray a 9-inch pie plate with nonstick cooking spray.

2 In a medium saucepan, combine the nonfat milk powder and flour. Whisk in the liquid milk until smooth. Bring to a simmer over medium heat. Add the jalapeño, chili powder, sugar, and salt, and cook, stirring constantly, until the mixture is thick enough to coat the back of a spoon, about 3 minutes.

3 In a small bowl, whisk the egg whites. Whisk about ½ cup of the hot milk mixture into the egg whites.

4 Remove the saucepan from the heat and stir the warmed egg-white mixture back into the milk mixture. Stir in the corn kernels, creamed corn, and cilantro. Spoon the corn mixture into the pie plate.

5 Bake until the pudding is set and the top is golden brown, about 35 minutes. *Makes 4 servings*

Corn Pudding with Roasted Peppers & Scallions Omit the cilantro and stir in ½ cup chopped roasted red or yellow peppers and 3 tablespoons sliced scallions in step 4.

Baked Pinto Beans

Most baked bean recipes start off with a little bit of bacon or fatback. To capture that smokiness without the saturated fat, we've added a touch of liquid smoke instead.

1 tablespoon olive oil
1 large onion, finely chopped
2 green bell peppers, cut into ½-inch chunks
5 cloves garlic, minced
2 cans (19 ounces each) pinto beans, rinsed and drained
1 can (14½ ounces) crushed tomatoes
2 teaspoons grated orange zest
1¼ cups water
3 tablespoons dark brown sugar
2 tablespoons molasses
2 teaspoons Dijon mustard
1 teaspoon ground ginger
½ teaspoon salt
½ teaspoon liquid smoke seasoning

1 Preheat the oven to 400°F. In a large nonstick ovenproof skillet, heat the oil over medium heat. Add the onion, bell peppers, and garlic, and cook, stirring frequently, until the onion is tender, about 7 minutes.

2 Stir in the beans, tomatoes, orange zest, water, brown sugar, molasses, mustard, ginger, salt, and liquid smoke, and bring to a boil.

3 Cover, place in the oven, and bake until the beans are richly flavored, about 15 minutes. Uncover and bake until the mixture is thick and the beans are very soft, about 10 minutes *Makes 6 servings*

F.Y.I.

Liquid smoke is a seasoning made from water and concentrated smoke. A small amount of liquid smoke adds a flavor that mimics that found in smoked meats, so you can give a traditional taste to dishes such as split pea soup, braised greens, and baked beans without using any fatty meat. The most common liquid smoke is made from hickory, but other woods are available, such as mesquite.

KITCHEN *tip*

Sweet potatoes can be "baked" in a microwave oven, just like regular potatoes. The difference, however, is that the higher moisture and sugar content of a standard-issue orange-fleshed sweet potato means that it cooks much faster in the microwave than regular baked potatoes. If your oven provides instructions for baking sweet potatoes specifically, then follow them. If not, try cooking the sweet potatoes for about one-half to two-thirds the amount of time it ordinarily takes to microwave regular baking potatoes.

Maple Sweet Potatoes with Cranberries

For this all-American side dish, sweet potatoes (native to this continent) are cooked with two other distinctly American ingredients: maple syrup and cranberries.

> 2 pounds sweet potatoes
> 4 teaspoons olive oil
> 3 cloves garlic, thinly sliced
> ¼ cup maple syrup
> 1 teaspoon grated lemon zest
> ¾ teaspoon salt
> ½ teaspoon pepper
> ½ cup dried cranberries

1 Preheat the oven to 450°F. Bake the sweet potatoes until tender, about 45 minutes. When cool enough to handle, peel and thickly slice.

2 In a large nonstick skillet, heat the oil over low heat. Add the garlic and cook until tender, about 1 minute. Add the maple syrup, lemon zest, salt, and pepper, and bring to a boil.

3 Add the sweet potatoes and dried cranberries, and toss until the potatoes are well coated. *Makes 6 servings*

Sweet & Sour Red Cabbage

Not your everyday sweet-and-sour cabbage dish, this sautéed vegetable mixture is highlighted with minced fresh ginger. Use another carrot if parsnips are not available.

2 teaspoons olive oil
1 large red onion, cut into small chunks
3 cloves garlic, minced
1 tablespoon minced fresh ginger
2 carrots, halved lengthwise and thinly sliced crosswise
1 parsnip, halved lengthwise and thinly sliced crosswise
6 cups thickly shredded red cabbage
3 tablespoons sugar
½ teaspoon salt
¼ cup red wine vinegar

1 In a nonstick Dutch oven, heat the oil over low heat. Add the onion, garlic, and ginger, and cook, stirring frequently, until the onion is golden brown, about 7 minutes.

2 Add the carrots and parsnip, and cook, stirring frequently, until the carrots are crisp-tender, about 5 minutes.

3 Stir in the cabbage, sugar, and salt. Cover and cook, stirring occasionally, until the cabbage is wilted, about 10 minutes.

4 Uncover, add the vinegar, increase the heat to medium-high, and cook, uncovered, until the cabbage is well coated, about 3 minutes. Serve warm or at room temperature. *Makes 4 servings*

F.Y.I.

Red cabbage is a member of the cruciferous family (which includes cabbage, Brussels sprouts, kale, broccoli, mustard greens, radishes, bok choy, and cauliflower) and as such supplies ample amounts of phytochemical compounds called indoles, which may have the potential to fight cancer. Cruciferous vegetables also contain sulforaphane, a phytochemical discovered by a team of researchers at Johns Hopkins University. Laboratory studies show that sulforaphane may increase the production of an enzyme that helps remove carcinogens from cells.

Garlic-Herb Sautéed Cherry Tomatoes

You could also make this dish with the smaller grape tomatoes. Serve the tomatoes as a vegetable side dish, or toss them with pasta for a light vegetarian main dish.

1 cup water
4 cloves garlic, minced
4 cups cherry tomatoes
½ teaspoon salt
¼ teaspoon oregano
2 tablespoons balsamic vinegar
2 scallions, thinly sliced
¼ cup chopped fresh basil

1 In a large nonstick skillet, bring ½ cup of the water and the garlic to a boil over medium heat. Boil until the garlic is tender, about 1 minute.

2 Add the tomatoes, salt, and oregano, and cook until the tomatoes begin to collapse, about 4 minutes.

3 Add the remaining ½ cup water, the vinegar, scallions, and basil, and toss well to combine. *Makes 4 servings*

Scallops with Sautéed Tomatoes To convert this vegetable side dish to a protein-rich main dish, in step 3, use ½ cup orange juice instead of the water and add the remaining ingredients as directed. Then add 1 pound bay scallops and simmer until just opaque, about 3 minutes.

KITCHEN *tip*

Here's a good trick for cutting up fresh basil leaves. Take all of the leaves and stack them up. With the long side of the stack facing you, roll the leaves into a cylinder. Then, with a sharp knife, cut the cylinder crosswise into thin shreds. In French cooking, this technique is called making a *chiffonade* (it literally translates as made of rags). You can leave the shreds as is or chop them even finer, depending on what the recipe calls for.

HOMEMADE

savory shakes

Though shakes are usually thought of as sweet, they also make good savory snacks. The Indian-Spiced Buttermilk is based on a drink called *lhassi*, which is the East Indian version of a smoothie. It's usually made with soured milk or yogurt, can be sweet or savory, and often contains typically Indian spices, such as cumin and coriander. The Carrot, Apple & Ginger Shake hovers intriguingly between sweet and savory, with the tart apple underscoring the natural sweetness of the carrot juice. And the Yogurt-Cucumber Shake has distinctly savory flavors, including fresh dill, making it reminiscent of Scandinavian cuisine.

Indian-Spiced Buttermilk

½ teaspoon cumin
½ teaspoon coriander
¾ cup buttermilk
2 tablespoons fresh mint leaves
2 teaspoons honey
2 ice cubes

1 In a small, ungreased skillet, toast the cumin over medium-low heat until fragrant and slightly darker in color, 1 to 2 minutes. Immediately transfer to a small plate or bowl so it won't keep cooking.
2 In a blender, combine the toasted cumin, coriander, buttermilk, mint, honey, and ice cubes, and puree until thick. *Makes 1 serving*

PER SERVING: 159 CALORIES, 4G TOTAL FAT (1.2G SATURATED), 6MG CHOLESTEROL, 2G DIETARY FIBER, 26G CARBOHYDRATE, 8G PROTEIN, 212MG SODIUM. **GOOD SOURCE OF:** CALCIUM, MAGNESIUM, POTASSIUM, RIBOFLAVIN, VITAMIN B_{12}

Carrot, Apple & Ginger Shake

⅔ cup carrot juice
½ cup peeled apple wedges
1 tablespoon grated fresh ginger
1 teaspoon fresh lemon juice
3 ice cubes

In a blender, combine all of the ingredients and puree until thick and smooth. *Makes 1 serving*

PER SERVING: 104 CALORIES, 0.5G TOTAL FAT (0.1G SATURATED), 0MG CHOLESTEROL, 3G DIETARY FIBER, 25G CARBOHYDRATE, 1.7G PROTEIN, 46MG SODIUM. **GOOD SOURCE OF:** BETA CAROTENE, POTASSIUM, THIAMIN, VITAMIN B_6, VITAMIN C

Yogurt-Cucumber Shake

½ cup plain fat-free yogurt
½ cup peeled, seeded, and sliced cucumber
3 tablespoons minced fresh dill
3 tablespoons minced red onion
¼ teaspoon salt
2 ice cubes

In a blender, combine all of the ingredients and puree until thick and smooth. *Makes 1 serving*

PER SERVING: 69 CALORIES, 0.2G TOTAL FAT (0G SATURATED), 3MG CHOLESTEROL, 1G DIETARY FIBER, 14G CARBOHYDRATE, 6G PROTEIN, 652MG SODIUM. **GOOD SOURCE OF:** CALCIUM

per serving	
calories	101
total fat	2.4g
saturated fat	0.3g
cholesterol	0mg
dietary fiber	4g
carbohydrate	18g
protein	4g
sodium	608mg

good source of: fiber, vitamin C

Sugar Snap Peas with Basil & Tomatoes

Although the whole pod of a sugar snap pea is theoretically edible, there is a tough string that runs down one or both sides of the pod. Larger (older) peas will have the string on both sides, smaller peas usually just on one side.

2 teaspoons olive oil
3 cloves garlic, slivered
¾ pound sugar snap peas, strings removed
1 can (14½ ounces) stewed tomatoes, drained
¼ cup minced fresh basil
½ teaspoon salt

1 In a large nonstick skillet, heat the oil over medium heat. Add the garlic and cook until tender, about 1 minute.

2 Add the sugar snaps, tomatoes, basil, and salt, and cook, stirring frequently until the peas are tender, about 4 minutes. *Makes 4 servings*

Lemony Mushrooms

These mushrooms can be served hot as a side dish, or chilled as a fine salad. Or if you drain the cooked mushrooms and chop them up a bit, they make a great sandwich topping.

per serving	
calories	76
total fat	2.3g
saturated fat	0.3g
cholesterol	0mg
dietary fiber	2g
carbohydrate	9g
protein	6g
sodium	376mg

good source of: potassium, vitamin C

2 teaspoons olive oil
3 cloves garlic, minced
⅔ cup chicken broth, homemade (*page 25*) or
    reduced-sodium canned
1½ pounds mushrooms, quartered
1 teaspoon grated lemon zest
3 tablespoons fresh lemon juice
½ teaspoon salt
¼ teaspoon pepper

1 In a large nonstick skillet, heat the oil over low heat. Add the garlic and cook until tender, about 1 minute. Add the broth and bring to a boil.

2 Add the mushrooms and cook, stirring frequently, until the mushrooms are tender, about 7 minutes.

3 Remove from the heat and stir in the lemon zest, lemon juice, salt, and pepper. Serve hot, at room temperature, or chilled. ***Makes 4 servings***

KITCHEN *tip*

The zest of citrus fruits is the thin, colored portion of the peel (as opposed to the spongy white layer) that contains the fruit's aromatic oils. Many recipes call for either strips of zest or grated zest. Strips can be removed with a vegetable peeler or small sharp knife. To grate citrus zest, however, it's best to have a specialized tool called a zester. There are several different types: One is a small tool with 5 small sharp-edged holes that you drag across the citrus peel, thus removing long thin strings of zest. Another tool resembles a woodworking rasp: It's a sturdy strip of stainless steel pierced with razor-sharp grating holes.

Sesame Asparagus & Snow Peas

Toasted sesame seeds and toasted sesame seed oil give a rich, dark flavor to this steamed vegetable dish.

per serving	
calories	61
total fat	2.4g
saturated fat	0.4g
cholesterol	0mg
dietary fiber	3g
carbohydrate	8g
protein	4g
sodium	301mg

good source of: beta carotene, fiber, folate, riboflavin, thiamin, vitamin B$_6$, vitamin C, vitamin E

2 teaspoons hulled sesame seeds
1¼ pounds asparagus, cut into 2-inch lengths
6 ounces snow peas, strings removed
1 red bell pepper, cut into thin strips
1 teaspoon dark sesame oil
½ teaspoon salt

1 In a small, ungreased skillet, toast the sesame seeds over low heat, stirring frequently, until golden brown, about 3 minutes. Transfer to a plate to prevent further cooking.

2 In a vegetable steamer, cook the asparagus and snow peas until tender, about 4 minutes.

3 Transfer to a large bowl. Add the bell pepper, sesame oil, and salt, and toss to combine. Sprinkle with the toasted sesame seeds. ***Makes 4 servings***

Pasta with Asparagus & Snow Peas Omit the sesame seeds. Cook 8 ounces of linguine or fettuccine. In step 3, increase the sesame oil to 1 tablespoon. Add the cooked pasta to the bowl of vegetables. Sprinkle with 2 tablespoons grated Parmesan and toss everything together.

Recipes for Weight Loss

Vegetarian Dutch Lettuce

While traditional Dutch lettuce is made with a bacon fat-based dressing, this healthful version uses liquid smoke and meaty dried mushrooms to give the impression of bacon but with none of the saturated fat.

1/2 cup dried porcini or shiitake mushrooms (1/2 ounce)

1 1/3 cups boiling water

1 1/2 pounds small red potatoes

1 head of romaine lettuce, cut into bite-size pieces (12 cups)

1 tablespoon olive oil

1 small red onion, finely chopped

3 tablespoons red wine vinegar

3/4 teaspoon salt

1/4 teaspoon liquid smoke seasoning

1 tablespoon Dijon mustard

1 1/2 teaspoons cornstarch blended with 1 tablespoon water

1 In a small heatproof bowl, combine the dried mushrooms and the boiling water, and let stand for 20 minutes or until softened. Reserving the soaking liquid, scoop out the dried mushrooms and coarsely chop. Strain the soaking liquid through a coffee filter or a paper towel-lined sieve.

2 Meanwhile, in a large pot of boiling water, cook the potatoes until tender, about 25 minutes. Drain and cut into 1/2-inch chunks. Transfer the potatoes to a large bowl. Add the lettuce and toss to combine.

3 In a large skillet, heat the oil over medium heat. Add the onion and cook, stirring occasionally, until tender, about 5 minutes. Add the mushrooms, reserved soaking liquid, vinegar, salt, and liquid smoke, and bring to a boil. Cook for 2 minutes.

4 Stir in the mustard and cornstarch mixture and boil, stirring constantly, until the dressing is slightly thickened, about 1 minute. Pour the hot dressing over the lettuce and potatoes, and toss well to coat. ***Makes 6 servings***

KITCHEN *tip*

If you were to add cornstarch directly to a hot liquid, the starch granules that hit the liquid first would swell and turn into a gel, effectively forming a waterproof barrier around the rest of the cornstarch. The result? A lumpy sauce. To avoid this, the cornstarch should first be stirred into a small amount of cold liquid (usually in a ratio of about 1 part cornstarch to 2 or 3 parts water). This separates the starch granules so that they will all swell evenly, which is in fact how they "thicken" the liquid they are added to.

Spotlite recipe

Kasha with Mushrooms

Roasted, hulled buckwheat kernels that are either whole-grain or cracked into coarse, medium, or fine granulations are commonly known as kasha. Buckwheat is high in an essential amino acid called lysine—which is lacking in most plant foods. It is also an excellent source of magnesium. Enjoy the toasty flavor of buckwheat in this mushroomy side dish.

1 tablespoon olive oil
2 large onions, halved and thinly sliced
1 pound mushrooms, thinly sliced
¾ teaspoon salt
½ teaspoon pepper
1 cup whole-grain kasha
1¾ cups vegetable broth, homemade (*page 25*) or
    canned

1 In a large nonstick skillet, heat the oil over medium-high heat. Add the onions and cook, stirring frequently, until the onions are golden brown and tender, about 15 minutes.

2 Add the mushrooms, ¼ teaspoon of the salt, and the pepper, and cook, stirring frequently, until the mushrooms are tender, about 10 minutes.

3 Meanwhile, place the kasha in another large skillet and cook over medium heat, stirring frequently, until lightly toasted, about 5 minutes.

4 Add the broth and the remaining ½ teaspoon salt to the kasha, and bring to a boil. Add the onion-mushroom mixture to the kasha, cover, and cook until the kasha is tender, about 10 minutes. Fluff with a fork before serving. ***Makes 4 servings***

PER SERVING 134 calories, 4.2g total fat (0.5g saturated), 0mg cholesterol, 4g dietary fiber, 21g carbohydrate, 7g protein, 878mg sodium
Good source of: **potassium**

Green Rice & Peas

Chopped cilantro and basil add lots of color and wonderful fresh flavors to this brown rice and green pea side dish.

1 tablespoon olive oil
4 cloves garlic, minced
2 tablespoons minced fresh ginger
¾ cup brown rice
⅔ cup chopped cilantro
⅔ cup chopped fresh basil
1¾ cups water
¾ teaspoon salt
⅔ cup frozen peas, thawed

KITCHEN*tip*

When using leafy fresh herbs—such as basil, cilantro, and mint— in a cooked dish, add them at the last minute so the freshness of their flavors is retained.

1 In a medium saucepan, heat the oil over medium heat. Add the garlic and ginger, and cook until tender, about 2 minutes.

2 Add the brown rice, ⅓ cup of the cilantro, and ⅓ cup of the basil, stirring to coat. Add the water and salt, and bring to a boil. Reduce to a simmer, cover, and cook until the rice is tender, 45 minutes to 1 hour.

3 Stir in the peas and cook until heated through, about 1 minute. Remove from the heat and stir in the remaining ⅓ cup cilantro and ⅓ cup basil.
Makes 4 servings

Cilantro Rice with Ham & Corn Omit the basil and increase the cilantro to 1 cup. In step 2, add ½ cup of the cilantro. In step 3, substitute frozen corn for the peas and add ½ cup diced reduced-sodium ham. Just before serving, stir in the remaining ½ cup cilantro.

Bulgur with Asparagus & Peas

Here's a take-off on tabbouleh, a Middle Eastern salad made with bulgur, a lemony dressing, and lots of parsley. We've used mint instead, and added steamed asparagus and green peas.

1¼ cups bulgur
3½ cups boiling water
3 tablespoons fresh lemon juice
1 tablespoons olive oil
¾ teaspoon salt
½ teaspoon pepper
½ pound asparagus spears, cut into 2-inch lengths
1 cup frozen peas, thawed
¼ cup chopped fresh mint
2 scallions, thinly sliced

1 In a large heatproof bowl, combine the bulgur and boiling water. Let stand until the bulgur has softened, about 30 minutes. Drain the bulgur and squeeze it dry.

2 In a large bowl, whisk together the lemon juice, oil, salt, and pepper. Add the drained bulgur and fluff with a fork.

3 In a vegetable steamer, cook the asparagus until tender, about 4 minutes. Add the asparagus and peas to the bulgur along with the mint and scallions, and toss to combine. Serve at room temperature or chilled. *Makes 6 servings*

per serving	
calories	154
total fat	2.8g
saturated fat	0.4g
cholesterol	0mg
dietary fiber	8g
carbohydrate	29g
protein	6g
sodium	341mg

good source of: fiber, folate

KITCHEN *tip*

Bulgur (wheat kernels that have been steamed and then crushed) is "cooked" by soaking it in hot or boiling water to soften it. Instead of trying to calculate exactly how much water will be absorbed by the bulgur (the amount required can vary with the age and storage of the bulgur), use a little more water than the bulgur will need. Once the bulgur has softened, drain off any excess liquid and squeeze the bulgur as dry as possible. One of the main reasons for that (in addition to keeping the bulgur from tasting waterlogged) is to allow the bulgur to absorb any flavored liquid—such as lemon juice, vinegar, or broth—that's being used in the recipe.

Peppery Pumpkin Risotto

A true Italian risotto would be made with a starchy type of rice called Arborio. Here we've used brown rice instead, which adds more fiber and makes a risotto with a chewier texture.

1 tablespoon olive oil
1 small onion, finely chopped
1¼ cups brown rice
⅔ cup dry white wine
2 cups carrot juice
2 cups water
¾ cup canned unsweetened pumpkin puree
1 teaspoon salt
½ teaspoon rubbed sage
3 tablespoons grated Parmesan cheese
½ teaspoon pepper

1 In a medium, heavy-bottomed saucepan, heat the oil over medium heat. Add the onion and cook until golden brown, about 7 minutes. Add the rice, stirring to coat. Add the wine and cook until absorbed, about 4 minutes.

2 Meanwhile, in a separate saucepan, heat the carrot juice and water over medium heat until warm. Keep warm over low heat.

3 Stir 2 cups of the warm carrot juice mixture into the rice and cook, uncovered, over low heat, stirring occasionally, until the liquid has been completely absorbed, about 20 minutes.

4 Add the remaining 2 cups warm carrot juice mixture, the pumpkin puree, salt, and sage, and cook over low heat, stirring frequently, until almost all liquid has been absorbed (the rice should be tender, but not mushy), about 25 minutes. Remove from the heat and stir in the Parmesan and pepper.
Makes 6 servings

Quinoa with Peanuts & Dried Cherries

Quinoa can sometimes have a very slightly bitter taste, but toasting the grain in an ungreased skillet before cooking it removes any bitterness.

2 teaspoons olive oil
1 large onion, finely chopped
2 cloves garlic, minced
1 cup quinoa
1 cup boiling water
¾ teaspoon salt
½ teaspoon pepper
¼ teaspoon rosemary, minced
¼ cup dried cherries
3 tablespoons coarsely chopped dry-roasted peanuts

1 In a large nonstick saucepan, heat the oil over low heat. Add the onion and garlic, and cook, stirring frequently, until the onion is golden brown, about 7 minutes.

2 Meanwhile, place the quinoa in a large ungreased skillet over medium heat and cook, stirring occasionally, until lightly toasted, about 5 minutes.

3 Add the quinoa to the onion mixture. Stir in the boiling water, salt, pepper, and rosemary. Return to a boil, cover, and gently boil 10 minutes. Uncover and cook, stirring occasionally, until the liquid has been absorbed and the quinoa is tender, 10 to 12 minutes.

4 Remove from the heat and stir in the cherries and peanuts. Serve hot, at room temperature, or chilled. *Makes 6 servings*

F.Y.I.

An ancient grainlike product from South America that has recently been "rediscovered" in this country, quinoa (pronounced KEEN-wah) is not a true grain (neither is buckwheat or amaranth), but it looks like one and has similar uses. It is related to leafy vegetables such as Swiss chard and spinach. Quinoa grains are about the same size as millet, but are flattened, with a pointed, oval shape. As quinoa cooks, the external germ, which forms a band around each grain, spirals out, forming a tiny crescent-shaped "tail." Although the grain itself is soft and creamy, the tail is crunchy, providing a unique textural complement. Quinoa is available in health-food stores and in many large supermarkets.

Grilled New Potato Salad

Adding the grilled new potatoes to the dressing while they're still warm makes them extra flavorful.

2 pounds small red potatoes, halved
½ cup dry white wine
3 tablespoons distilled white vinegar
2 tablespoons Dijon mustard
¼ teaspoon salt
1 small red onion, finely chopped
2 stalks celery, thinly sliced
1 tablespoon capers, rinsed and drained
2 red bell peppers, cut lengthwise into flat panels

1 Preheat the grill. Spray a grill topper with nonstick cooking spray.

2 In a large pot of boiling water, cook the potatoes until firm-tender, about 10 minutes. Drain.

3 Meanwhile, in a large bowl, whisk together the wine, vinegar, mustard, and salt. Stir in the onion, celery, and capers. Set aside.

4 Grill the potatoes and bell pepper panels, skin-side down, on the grill topper, covered, until the pepper skins are charred and the potatoes are cooked through, about 10 minutes. When cool enough to handle, peel the peppers and cut into ½-inch-wide strips. Add the peppers to the bowl of dressing.

5 Halve the potatoes again (into quarters) and add to the bowl of dressing. Toss to combine. Serve at room temperature or chilled. ***Makes 4 servings***

HOMEMADE
fat-free dressings

In a regular salad dressing, oil serves two purposes: It helps the dressing coat the greens and it tempers the acidity of an ingredient such as lemon juice or vinegar. Each of the salad dressings here was made a different thickener, each of which mimics the coating and acid-balancing abilities of oil. In the Balsamic Vinaigrette, the thickener is cornstarch, which when combined with a liquid and heated turns thick and glossy. In the spicy, sweet-tart Pineapple-Tarragon Dressing, the thickening agent is fruit pectin, which is used in canning to give body to jams and jellies. And finally, in the Carrot-Orange Dressing, the thickener is gelatin, which is dissolved and then combined with the other dressing ingredients. Each of the dressings is technically (as far as labeling laws go) fat-free, but each of them has a fractional amount of unsaturated fat, which comes from the mustard and the cayenne (both of which contain a bit of oil from their seeds).

Fat-Free Balsamic Vinaigrette

2 teaspoons cornstarch
¼ cup water
½ cup balsamic vinegar
2 shallots, minced (¼ cup) or minced whites of 2 scallions
4 teaspoons Dijon mustard
1 tablespoon honey

ı In a small saucepan, whisk together the cornstarch and water until smooth. Bring to a boil over medium heat and cook until thickened, about ı minute.
2 Off the heat, whisk in the vinegar, shallots, mustard, and honey until smooth. Let cool to room temperature and refrigerate. *Makes ı cup*

PER 2 TABLESPOONS: 25 CALORIES, 0.3G TOTAL FAT (0G SATURATED), 0MG CHOLESTEROL, 0G DIETARY FIBER, 6G CARBOHYDRATE, 0G PROTEIN, 67MG SODIUM

Fat-Free Pineapple-Tarragon Dressing

¾ cup unsweetened pineapple juice
¼ cup fresh lime juice
¼ cup sugar
1½ teaspoons tarragon
¾ teaspoon salt
¼ teaspoon cayenne pepper
1 tablespoon granulated fruit pectin

ı In a small saucepan, combine the pineapple juice, lime juice, sugar, tarragon, salt, and cayenne. Bring to a boil over medium heat.
2 Stir in the pectin, return to a boil, and cook, stirring constantly, for ı minute. Let cool to room temperature and refrigerate. *Makes ı cup*

PER 2 TABLESPOONS: 48 CALORIES, 0.1G TOTAL FAT (0G SATURATED), 0MG CHOLESTEROL, 0G DIETARY FIBER, 12G CARBOHYDRATE, 0G PROTEIN, 219MG SODIUM

Carrot-Orange Dressing

¾ teaspoon unflavored gelatin
2 tablespoons water
¾ cup carrot juice
3 tablespoons orange juice
4 teaspoons white wine vinegar
¼ teaspoon salt
⅛ teaspoon cayenne pepper

ı In a small heatproof bowl, sprinkle the gelatin over the water and let stand until the gelatin has softened, about 2 minutes. Place the bowl in a pan of simmering water and heat until the gelatin has dissolved, about 2 minutes. Remove from the pan and let the gelatin cool to room temperature.
2 In a small bowl, or a jar with a tight-fitting lid, combine the cooled gelatin, the carrot juice, orange juice, vinegar, salt, and cayenne. Whisk or shake to combine. Refrigerate for about ı hour or until slightly syrupy.
3 Store in the refrigerator, but bring back to room temperature before using or the dressing will be too thick. *Makes ı cup*

PER ¼ CUP: 26 CALORIES, 0.1G TOTAL FAT (0G SATURATED), 0MG CHOLESTEROL, 0G DIETARY FIBER, 5G CARBOHYDRATE, 1G PROTEIN, 159MG SODIUM. **GOOD SOURCE OF:** BETA CAROTENE

Coleslaw

Plain fat-free yogurt takes the place of most of the mayonnaise in this classic dish.

1 cup plain fat-free yogurt
2 tablespoons light mayonnaise
3 tablespoons fresh lemon juice
2 tablespoons Dijon mustard
1 tablespoon distilled white vinegar
1 tablespoon sugar
¾ teaspoon salt
½ teaspoon pepper
1 small head green cabbage (1¼ pounds), finely shredded
4 carrots, shredded
1 red bell pepper, cut into thin slivers

1 Spoon the yogurt into a paper coffee filter or paper towel-lined sieve and drain off the excess liquid for 2 minutes.

2 In a large bowl, whisk together the yogurt and mayonnaise until smooth. Add the lemon juice, mustard, vinegar, sugar, salt, and pepper, and whisk to combine. Add the cabbage, carrots, and bell pepper, and toss to combine.

3 Refrigerate for at least 1 hour before serving. *Makes 8 servings*

Cabbage & Apple Slaw Omit the carrots. Add 2 unpeeled, thinly sliced apples (1 red and 1 green, for color) and ¼ cup coarsely chopped walnuts.

KITCHEN *tip*

To get the most juice out of a lemon, roll the lemon back and forth on the countertop with the palm of your hand, pressing on the lemon. This helps breaks down the pulp and makes the lemon easier to juice.

Tomato & Cannellini Salad with Roasted Garlic Dressing

Roasting mellows the garlic's pungency, and the soft cooked garlic adds both texture and flavor to the herbed dressing for this bean and tomato salad.

1 medium head of garlic (about 3 ounces)
1½ teaspoons olive oil
¼ cup minced shallots or scallion whites
¾ teaspoon rubbed sage
3 cups diced plum tomatoes
⅓ cup diced celery
⅓ cup diced red onion
3 tablespoons chopped parsley
3 tablespoons minced chives or scallion greens
2 tablespoons fresh lemon juice
1 tablespoon balsamic vinegar
1 can (19 ounces) cannellini beans, rinsed and drained

1 Preheat the oven to 375°F. Wrap the garlic in foil, place on a baking sheet, and bake until the garlic is soft, about 30 minutes. When cool enough to handle, unwrap the head of garlic, cut off the stem end, and squeeze out the soft garlic inside. Set aside.

2 In a small nonstick skillet, heat the oil over low heat. Add the shallots and cook, stirring frequently, until soft, about 3 minutes. Add the sage, stirring to coat.

3 Remove from the heat and transfer to a large bowl. Stir in the roasted garlic pulp. Then stir in the tomatoes, celery, onion, parsley, chives, lemon juice, and vinegar. Add the beans and toss gently to combine. *Makes 4 servings*

Tomato-Bean Salad with Orzo Omit the sage, celery, and parsley. Add 2 cups cooked orzo and ⅔ cup of crumbled feta cheese when adding the tomatoes. Serve at room temperature or chilled.

Recipes for Weight Loss

per serving	
calories	112
total fat	3.4g
saturated fat	0.4g
cholesterol	3mg
dietary fiber	5g
carbohydrate	19g
protein	5g
sodium	204mg

good source of: beta carotene, fiber, folate, magnesium, niacin, potassium, riboflavin, thiamin, vitamin B$_6$, vitamin C, vitamin E

Vegetable Slaw with Lemon-Mustard Dressing

All the shredded vegetables for this tasty slaw can be prepared in a food processor fitted with the shredding blade. Shred them separately and pour off any excess liquid from the shredded summer squash and zucchini so it won't water down the dressing.

> 3 tablespoons fresh lemon juice
> 2 tablespoons light mayonnaise
> ½ cup plain fat-free yogurt
> 1 tablespoon Dijon mustard
> ½ teaspoon pepper
> 4 medium carrots, shredded
> 2 medium yellow summer squash, shredded
> 2 medium zucchini, shredded

In a salad bowl, whisk together the lemon juice, mayonnaise, yogurt, mustard, and pepper. Add the carrots, yellow squash, and zucchini, and toss to coat well. ***Makes 4 servings***

Hot Berry Sundaes

The blueberries and raspberries in this warm ice-cream topping supply health-giving antioxidants you won't find in any chocolate sauce! The berry topping is also delicious over slices of plain cake.

⅓ cup raspberry fruit spread
2 tablespoons pure maple syrup
1 tablespoon fresh lemon juice
2 cups fresh or unsweetened frozen blueberries
1 cup fresh or unsweetened frozen raspberries
1 pint low-fat frozen vanilla yogurt

1 Preheat the oven to 400°F.

2 In a medium bowl, stir together the fruit spread, maple syrup, and lemon juice. Add the berries and mix gently. Scrape the mixture into a 9-inch pie plate.

3 Bake the berries for 15 minutes, or until hot and bubbly (frozen berries will take a few minutes longer). Scoop the frozen yogurt into dessert dishes and top with the hot berry mixture. ***Makes 4 servings***

F.Y.I.

Not only are berries rich in fiber, vitamin C, and flavor, but they also contain phyto-chemicals, such as ellagic acid and anthocyanins, which are under review for the potential to prevent certain diseases. Population studies show that a high intake of fruit and vegetables may help to lower the risk for certain types of cancer and heart disease.

Spotlite recipe

Mango & Dried Fruit Compote

Mangoes, delicious tropical fruits with a lush texture and beautiful color, are also rich in nutrients. Mangoes have good amounts of soluble fiber, vitamin C, and vitamin E. Their orange flesh also indicates the presence of beta carotene as well as small amounts of another carotenoid, beta cryptoxanthin. In this marvelous fruit compote, fresh mangoes are paired with stewed dried fruit. Serve it for dessert or for breakfast as a topping for waffles or pancakes. If you make the compote ahead of time, add the fresh fruits just before serving.

1 cup dried peaches, halved
1 cup dried apricots
1 cup pitted dried plums (prunes), halved
Half a lemon, sliced, seeds removed, and slices cut into half-moons
2 cups pineapple juice
1 cup water
3 tablespoons dark brown sugar
1 cinnamon stick
J teaspoon ground cloves
2 mangoes, peeled and cut into chunks

1 In a large nonstick saucepan, combine the dried fruit, lemon slices, pineapple juice, water, brown sugar, cinnamon stick, and cloves. Stir to dissolve the sugar. Cover and bring to a boil over high heat. Reduce the heat to medium-low and simmer, stirring occasionally, until the fruit is very soft, 15 to 20 minutes.

2 Remove from the heat and pour the dried fruit mixture into a serving bowl. Cool to warm (or place in the freezer to quick-chill), then remove and discard the cinnamon stick.

3 Stir the mango into the fruit mixture. Serve at room temperature or lightly chilled. *Makes 8 servings*

PER SERVING 236 calories, 0.6g total fat (0.1g saturated), 0mg cholesterol, 7g dietary fiber, 62g carbohydrate, 3g protein, 8mg sodium
Good source of: beta carotene, fiber, niacin, potassium, vitamin B$_6$, vitamin C

Strawberry Long Cake

Everyone's heard of strawberry shortcake, so why not a strawberry long cake? Perfect for company, this light chocolate cake roll with creamy strawberry filling should impress your guests with its low-calorie profile as well as its looks.

per serving	
calories	179
total fat	3.3g
saturated fat	1.6g
cholesterol	59mg
dietary fiber	1g
carbohydrate	32g
protein	6g
sodium	126mg

good source of:
selenium, vitamin C

½ cup flour
¼ cup unsweetened cocoa powder
2 tablespoons cornstarch
¾ teaspoon baking powder
¼ teaspoon salt
3 large eggs
2 large egg whites
1 tablespoon water
⅔ cup packed light brown sugar
1 teaspoon vanilla extract
Confectioners' sugar, for dusting
1 cup part-skim ricotta cheese
1 tablespoon honey
½ cup strawberry jelly
2 cups chopped strawberries

1 Preheat the oven to 400°F. Line a 10 x 15-inch jelly-roll pan with wax paper. In a small bowl, stir together the flour, cocoa powder, cornstarch, baking powder, and salt. Set aside.

2 In a large bowl, with an electric mixer, beat the whole eggs, egg whites, and water until foamy. Gradually add the brown sugar, continuing to beat until very thick. Beat in the vanilla.

3 Fold the flour mixture into the egg mixture until blended. Spoon the batter into the jelly-roll pan, spreading it to the edges and smoothing the top. Bake 12 minutes, or until the top springs back when lightly touched.

4 Loosen the edges of the cake with a small metal spatula and invert onto a kitchen towel that's been lightly dusted with confectioners' sugar. Remove and discard the wax paper. Starting at one short end, roll the cake and towel up together. Cool 30 minutes on a wire rack.

5 In a small bowl, stir together the ricotta and honey. In a small saucepan, melt the jelly over low heat.

6 Unroll the cake. Spread the jelly over the cake, leaving a ½-inch border all around. Spread the ricotta over the jelly. Spread the strawberries over the ricotta. Starting at one short end, reroll cake. Place seam-side down on a cake plate. Refrigerate for at least 1 hour before serving. *Makes 12 servings*

Individual Pumpkin Soufflés

A soufflé is always something special. It's chemistry and magic all rolled into one.

per serving	
calories	115
total fat	0.2g
saturated fat	0g
cholesterol	0mg
dietary fiber	2g
carbohydrate	26g
protein	3g
sodium	46mg

good source of: beta carotene

1 cup fresh or frozen cranberries
9 tablespoons frozen apple juice concentrate, thawed
9 tablespoons water
1 tablespoon plus 1 teaspoon maple syrup
½ teaspoon fresh lemon juice
2 tablespoons sugar
2 tablespoons cornstarch
¼ teaspoon allspice
¼ teaspoon cinnamon
1 cup canned unsweetened pumpkin puree
4 large egg whites
¼ teaspoon cream of tartar

F.Y.I.

Though it may seem like a nuisance to cook these soufflés in individual ramekins, the psychology behind it is that portion size is clearly defined. This makes it easier to eat just one portion and save any leftovers for another day. Leftover pumpkin soufflés will of course not be light and airy, but the collapsed soufflés will taste like a delicious, dense baked pudding.

1 In a small nonaluminum saucepan, bring the cranberries and 3 tablespoons each of the apple juice concentrate and water to a boil over high heat; cook until the berries are soft. Reduce to medium and cook until syrupy, about 15 minutes. Off the heat, stir in the maple syrup and lemon juice.

2 Preheat the oven to 350°F. Spray six 6-ounce ramekins with nonstick cooking spray and dust with 1 tablespoon of the sugar.

3 Meanwhile, in a medium saucepan, whisk together the cornstarch and remaining 6 tablespoons each apple juice concentrate and water, and 1 tablespoon sugar. Whisking constantly, bring to a boil over medium heat and cook until the sauce thickens, about 5 minutes. Remove from the heat.

4 In a medium bowl, stir the allspice and cinnamon into the pumpkin puree. Stir in the thickened apple juice and mix well.

5 In another medium bowl, with an electric mixer, beat the egg whites until foamy. Add the cream of tartar and beat until stiff peaks form. Fold one-fourth of the beaten whites into the pumpkin mixture to lighten it, then gently fold in the remaining whites until just mixed.

6 Spoon the soufflé mixture into the prepared ramekins, filling them three-fourths full. Place in a roasting pan and pour in hot water to reach one-third of way up the sides of the ramekins. Bake 23 to 25 minutes, or until puffed and firm to the touch. Serve the soufflés with the cranberry sauce on top.
Makes 6 servings

Cinnamon-Raisin Bread Pudding

Comfort food at its best, with a hint of chocolate and delicious cinnamon-raisin bread. Serve the pudding warm, at room temperature, or chilled.

per serving	
calories	186
total fat	3.3g
saturated fat	1g
cholesterol	56mg
dietary fiber	1g
carbohydrate	33g
protein	8g
sodium	183mg

good source of:
riboflavin, vitamin B$_{12}$

6 slices cinnamon-raisin bread, lightly toasted
3 tablespoons unsweetened cocoa powder
2 cups low-fat (1%) milk
⅛ teaspoon almond extract
⅓ cup granulated sugar
2 teaspoons cornstarch
⅛ teaspoon nutmeg
⅛ teaspoon salt
2 large eggs
3 large egg whites
1 tablespoon confectioners' sugar

1　Preheat the oven to 350°F. Spray a shallow 7 x 11-inch baking dish with nonstick cooking spray. Arrange the bread in the baking dish, overlapping the slices slightly.

2　Place the cocoa powder in a small bowl and stir in ¼ cup of the milk until smooth. Stir in the remaining 1¾ cups milk, the almond extract, granulated sugar, cornstarch, nutmeg, and salt. Whisk in the whole eggs and egg whites until well combined.

3　Pour the mixture over the bread, cover with foil, and bake 25 minutes, or until the pudding is just set.

4　Dust the pudding with confectioners' sugar. ***Makes 8 servings***

per serving	
calories	212
total fat	0.2g
saturated fat	0g
cholesterol	0mg
dietary fiber	3g
carbohydrate	55g
protein	1.4g
sodium	299mg

KITCHEN *tip*

Not all apples are suitable for poaching. Some—McIntoshes for example—would simply fall apart and turn into applesauce instead of holding their shape. In addition to the apple types listed in the recipe, you could use Golden Delicious, Winesap, or Cortland apples.

Grape & Raspberry-Poached Apples

These poached apples make a wonderful herb-scented dessert, but they would also be a nice accompaniment to simple roast poultry or pork.

2 cups grape juice
⅓ cup seedless red raspberry jam
1 bay leaf
½ teaspoon rubbed sage
½ teaspoon salt
½ teaspoon pepper
¼ teaspoon allspice
4 large Granny Smith or Empire apples, peeled and
    quartered

1 In a medium saucepan, stir together the grape juice, jam, bay leaf, sage, salt, pepper, and allspice. Bring to a boil over medium heat.

2 Add the apples and reduce to a simmer. Cook, stirring frequently, until the apples are tender, about 15 minutes. With a slotted spoon, transfer the apples to a medium serving bowl and set aside.

3 Increase the heat to high under the poaching liquid and cook until reduced to a light syrup, 7 to 10 minutes.

4 Strain the syrup, discarding the bay leaf and sage. Cool the syrup to room temperature, then pour over the apples. Refrigerate until chilled. *Makes 4 servings*

Rosemary & Orange-Scented Apples In step 1, omit the sage, bay leaf, and allspice, and use ½ teaspoon minced rosemary and 4 strips of orange zest instead. Increase the pepper to ¾ teaspoon.

Spotlite recipe

Cocoa Brownies

²/₃ cup flour
½ cup unsweetened cocoa powder
2 tablespoons cornstarch
1 teaspoon baking powder
¼ teaspoon baking soda
¼ teaspoon salt
¾ cup sugar
½ cup apple butter
2 tablespoons walnut oil
2 large egg whites
1 teaspoon vanilla extract

1 Preheat the oven to 350°F. Spray an 8-inch square baking pan with non-stick cooking spray.

2 In a medium bowl, stir together the flour, cocoa powder, cornstarch, baking powder, baking soda, and salt.

3 In a large bowl, whisk together the sugar, apple butter, walnut oil, egg whites, and vanilla until well combined. Fold in the flour mixture.

4 Pour the batter into the pan and bake 16 to 20 minutes or until the cake begins to pull away from the sides of the pan but the center is still slightly soft. Cool in the pan on a wire rack, then cut into 12 brownies. ***Makes 12 brownies***

PER BROWNIE 132 calories, 2.8g total fat (0.5g saturated), omg cholesterol, 2g dietary fiber, 26g carbohydrate, 2g protein, 105mg sodium

Walnuts are a great ingredient in brownies, but they can bring with them quite a few grams of fat. So to get some of that walnut flavor without a lot of fat, we used walnut oil instead. For a relatively small amount of oil (only ½ teaspoon per brownie), the brownies have a nice nutty undertone. The toasted-nut flavor of the oil makes the brownies seem rich even though they have less than 3 grams of fat apiece. As a side benefit, walnut oil is a good source of alpha-linolenic acid, which is a precursor to heart-healthy omega-3 fatty acid.

F.Y.I.

In order to have a maximum of browned topping for a gratin (so everyone gets to have some), it's cooked in a shallow layer in a dish designed for the purpose. The so-called gratin dish is traditionally oval and made of porcelain, but there are also gratin dishes that are round or made of glass.

Winter Fruit Gratin

"Gratin" usually means a dish with a crust of melted cheese on top, but this French culinary term also describes a dish with a topping of heavy cream that's browned under the broiler. Here, meringue takes the place of cream as a topping for a low-fat, fiber-rich (from the pears and dried fruit) dessert.

½ cup apple juice
2 cups mixed dried fruit
1 teaspoon cinnamon
¼ cup golden raisins
1 tablespoon fresh lemon juice
3 cups firm-ripe, unpeeled Bartlett pear chunks (½ inch)
2 kiwifruit, peeled and cut into 1½-inch chunks
1 large egg white
¼ teaspoon cream of tartar
¼ cup sugar

1 Preheat the oven to 475°F. Lightly spray a gratin dish with nonstick cooking spray. In a medium saucepan, bring the apple juice to a boil over high heat. Add the dried fruit and return to a boil. Remove from the heat and stir in the cinnamon, raisins, and lemon juice. Set aside.

2 Transfer the contents of the saucepan to a large bowl. Add the pears and kiwi chunks, and stir gently to combine. Arrange the fruit in the gratin dish and set aside.

3 In a medium bowl, beat the egg white until frothy. Add the cream of tartar and beat to soft peaks. Gradually add the sugar 1 tablespoon at a time, and beat until stiff, shiny peaks form.

4 Spoon the meringue decoratively over the center of the fruit, allowing some of the fruit to peek out along the sides. Bake for 2 to 5 minutes, or until meringue is just beginning to brown. Serve warm. *Makes 6 servings*

Berry Cheesecake Mousse

This layered dessert is attractive served in large "balloon" wineglasses or goblets. You'll need glasses that hold at least 12 ounces.

½ teaspoon unflavored gelatin
¼ cup cold water
3 cups blueberries
2 tablespoons raspberry fruit spread
8 ounces fat-free cream cheese
¼ cup reduced-fat sour cream
½ cup sugar
½ cup low-fat (2%) evaporated milk, chilled

1 In a small, heatproof bowl, sprinkle the gelatin over the water and let stand until softened, about 2 minutes. Set the bowl in a pan of simmering water and heat until the gelatin dissolves, about 3 minutes. Set aside to cool to room temperature.

2 Set aside ¼ cup of the blueberries. In a medium bowl, combine the remaining blueberries and the fruit spread, tossing until well coated.

3 In a food processor, combine the cream cheese, 2 tablespoons of the sour cream, and ¼ cup of the sugar, and process until smooth.

4 In a medium bowl, with an electric mixer, beat the evaporated milk with the remaining 2 tablespoons sour cream and ¼ cup sugar until soft peaks form. Gradually beat in the cooled gelatin mixture.

5 Fold the cream cheese mixture into the evaporated milk mixture. Divide the blueberry-raspberry jam mixture among dessert bowls. Top with a layer of cheesecake mousse. Top the mousse with the reserved ¼ cup blueberries. Chill until set, about 1 hour. *Makes 4 servings*

per serving	
calories	275
total fat	3.1g
saturated fat	1.9g
cholesterol	15mg
dietary fiber	3g
carbohydrate	51g
protein	12g
sodium	363mg

good source of: calcium, riboflavin, vitamin B₁₂, vitamin C

per serving	
calories	100
total fat	0.5g
saturated fat	0.1g
cholesterol	0mg
dietary fiber	3g
carbohydrate	22g
protein	3g
sodium	6mg

good source of:
folate, potassium, thiamin, vitamin C

F.Y.I.

Strawberries provide dietary fiber and vitamin C (1 cup supplies 96% of the RDA for this antioxidant vitamin).

Fresh Fruit Gelatin

Between the fresh orange juice, sliced fresh strawberries, and canned mandarins, this light, refreshing dessert has heaps of vitamin C.

> 1 envelope unflavored gelatin
> 2 cups fresh orange juice
> 1 teaspoon grated orange zest
> ¼ teaspoon vanilla extract
> 1 cup canned juice-packed mandarin oranges, well
>   drained
> 1¼ cups sliced strawberries

1 In a small saucepan, sprinkle the gelatin over ½ cup of the orange juice. Warm the mixture over very low heat, stirring just until the gelatin has dissolved, then remove from the heat.

2 Transfer to a medium bowl. Stir in the remaining 1½ cups orange juice, the orange zest, and vanilla. Refrigerate until the mixture just starts to gel, about 1 hour.

3 In parfait glasses, spoon alternating layers of mandarin oranges, orange gelatin and strawberries. Repeat the layering, ending with the strawberries on top. Chill until set, 1 to 2 hours. *Makes 4 servings*

Pear-Cranberry Crumble

per serving	
calories	245
total fat	5.9g
saturated fat	0.8g
cholesterol	0mg
dietary fiber	5g
carbohydrate	49g
protein	2g
sodium	77mg

good source of: fiber

Cranberries give this crumble a pleasantly tangy edge. If your taste runs to sweeter things, increase the granulated sugar to ⅔ cup. When cranberries are in season, buy several bags and put them in the freezer to have on hand throughout the year. If you're using frozen cranberries, there's no need to thaw them before using.

½ cup granulated sugar
2 tablespoons cornstarch
½ teaspoon cinnamon
¼ teaspoon salt
⅛ teaspoon allspice
1 package (12 ounces) fresh or frozen cranberries
3 Bartlett pears, peeled, cored, and cut into 1-inch chunks
1 teaspoon vanilla extract
⅓ cup firmly packed light brown sugar
½ cup old-fashioned rolled oats
⅓ cup flour
3 tablespoons extra-light olive oil

1 Preheat the oven to 375°F. In a large bowl, stir together granulated sugar, cornstarch, cinnamon, salt, and allspice. Add cranberries, pears, and vanilla; stir to combine. Spoon into a 9-inch deep dish pie plate.

2 In a medium bowl, combine the brown sugar, oats, and flour. Pour in the olive oil and mix with a fork until evenly moistened. Sprinkle the oat mixture over the pear mixture and bake for 25 minutes, or until the filling is bubbly and the topping is golden brown. ***Makes 8 servings***

F.Y.I.

The cranberries, pears, and rolled oats in this crumble provide a good amount of cholesterol-lowering soluble fiber. In addition to its contribution to heart health, soluble fiber is valuable to appetite control: Soluble fiber absorbs water in the body, thus slowing down the digestive process and making you feel full longer.

Spotlite recipe

Pumpkin Cheesecake Puddings

Patrice Benneward, executive editor of *The Johns Hopkins Medical Letter, Health After 50*, wondered why she couldn't have all the delicious flavors of a pumpkin cheesecake without all the fat. So she started a series of experiments. She began by leaving out the butter-laden graham cracker crust (a big savings in saturated fat and calories). Then the trick was to get the pumpkin mixture to have body without all the cream cheese and eggs. This led to the addition of ricotta cheese and fat-free cottage cheese, and a major reduction in the egg yolks (extra egg whites take their place). The result was these delicious pumpkin cheesecake puddings. If you don't have 10 custard cups, you could also bake this pudding in a glass loaf pan; the baking time will be about 1 hour.

2 cups fat-free cottage cheese
1 cup part-skim ricotta cheese
2 tablespoons cornstarch
1 can (15 ounces) unsweetened pumpkin puree
½ cup packed light brown sugar
⅓ cup maple syrup
1 large egg
2 large egg whites
1 teaspoon cinnamon
½ teaspoon ground ginger
½ teaspoon salt
¼ teaspoon nutmeg

1 Preheat the oven to 325°F. In a food processor, combine the cottage cheese, ricotta, and cornstarch, and puree until very smooth, about 1 minute.

2 Add the pumpkin puree, brown sugar, maple syrup, egg, egg whites, cinnamon, ginger, salt, and nutmeg, and puree until well combined.

3 Spoon the mixture into ten 6-ounce custard cups or ramekins and bake until set, about 30 minutes. Serve chilled or at room temperature. *Makes 10 servings*

PER SERVING 163 calories, 2.5g total fat (1.4g saturated), 33mg cholesterol, 2g dietary fiber, 25g carbohydrate, 10g protein, 227mg sodium
Good source of: **beta carotene, riboflavin**

KITCHENtip

Once a pineapple has been picked, it will not continue to ripen, so it's important to choose one in prime condition at the market. Unfortunately, most of the traditional "secrets" to selecting this fruit are unreliable. You can't judge the fruit by its color (it can range from green to yellow-gold depending on the variety), or by thumping it to test its "soundness," or by pulling a crown leaf to see how loose it is. The fruit should be firm and plump, as well as heavy for its size, with fresh-looking green leaves. Look out for bruises or soft spots, especially at the base. Never buy a pineapple with a sour or fermented smell. Ultimately, your best guide to quality is a label or tag indicating that the pineapple was jet-shipped from the grower.

Grilled Pineapple with Maple Cream

If it seems like a lot of trouble to trim a fresh pineapple for this dessert, try to find already cored and sliced fresh pineapple in the supermarket.

½ cup fat-free sour cream
6 tablespoons maple sugar
1½ teaspoons ground ginger
¾ teaspoon cardamom
¾ teaspoon cinnamon
⅛ teaspoon ground cloves
4 cups fresh pineapple chunks

1 In a small bowl, stir together the sour cream and 2 tablespoons of the maple sugar. Refrigerate until serving time.

2 In a large bowl, stir together the remaining 4 tablespoons maple sugar, the ginger, cardamom, cinnamon, and cloves. Add the pineapple to the bowl and toss well to coat.

3 Preheat the broiler. Spray the broiler pan with nonstick cooking spray. Lift the pineapple from any juices that have accumulated in the bowl and thread the chunks onto 8 skewers.

4 Broil 4 to 6 inches from the heat for 6 minutes, turning the skewers over midway and brushing the pineapple with any juices in the bowl, until the pineapple has caramelized. Serve with the maple cream. *Makes 4 servings*

F.Y.I.

By making a pie with only a top crust, you reduce the total amount of fat from around 13 grams to a little over 6 grams. In addition, by using olive oil instead of butter in the crust, the saturated fat takes a nose-dive from more than 4 grams to 1.6 grams.

One-Crust Sour Cherry Pie

Sour cherries, or pie cherries, have a brief season. Buy them while you can and freeze what you don't use. However, you'll get wonderful results making this pie with bottled, canned, or frozen cherries. If you're using bottled, you'll need two 24-ounce bottles to get 5 cups of cherries.

1 cup flour
1 tablespoon plus ⅔ cup sugar
½ teaspoon salt
⅓ cup reduced-fat sour cream
3 tablespoons extra-light olive oil
2 tablespoons water
¼ cup cornstarch
5 cups pitted sour cherries
1 teaspoon grated lime zest
1 tablespoon fresh lime juice
⅛ teaspoon allspice

1 In a medium bowl, combine the flour, 1 tablespoon of the sugar, and the salt. In a small bowl, stir together the sour cream, oil, and water until well combined.

2 Make a well in the center of the flour mixture and spoon in the sour cream mixture. With a pastry blender or 2 knives, cut in the sour cream mixture until just combined. Gently shape the dough into a disk.

3 Preheat the oven to 375°F. In a large bowl, stir together the remaining ⅔ cup sugar and the cornstarch. Add the cherries, lime zest, lime juice, and allspice, and toss to combine. Transfer the cherry mixture to a 9-inch pie plate.

4 On a lightly floured surface, roll the dough out to a 12-inch round. Place the dough on top of the cherries. With your fingers, crimp the edges of the dough. With a sharp knife, cut several short slashes in the middle of the crust to act as steam vents. Transfer the pie to a jelly-roll pan.

5 Bake for 45 to 50 minutes or until bubbly and hot in the center. Serve the pie warm or at room temperature. **_Makes 8 servings_**

Breakfast Fruit Salad

You can make this salad a couple of hours ahead of time, but wait until just before serving to add the bananas so they don't get mushy.

3 tablespoons fresh lime juice
1 tablespoon honey
3 tablespoons minced fresh mint
½ teaspoon tarragon
2 cups cantaloupe chunks
1 cup pineapple chunks (fresh or canned)
1 cup cherries, halved and pitted
1 banana, thinly sliced

1   In a large bowl, whisk together the lime juice and honey. Add the mint and tarragon, and stir until combined.

2   Add the cantaloupe, pineapple, cherries, and banana, and toss gently. Serve the salad at room temperature or chilled. *Makes 4 servings*

KITCHEN *tip*

It might seem odd to use a savory herb in a fruit salad, but tarragon has sweet undertones that are brought out by the honey and the fruit. This is also true of mint, whose flavors allow it to work in both sweet and savory dishes.

per serving	
calories	137
total fat	0.6g
saturated fat	0.3g
cholesterol	0mg
dietary fiber	3g
carbohydrate	35g
protein	1g
sodium	4mg

good source of: potassium, vitamin B$_6$

Brown Sugar-Broiled Bananas

These broiled bananas would be delicious as part of a brunch. Or serve them for dessert, topped with a scoop of low-fat frozen yogurt.

    2 tablespoons light brown sugar
    2 tablespoons fresh lime juice
    ¼ teaspoon nutmeg
    ⅛ teaspoon allspice
    4 bananas (about 6 ounces each), halved lengthwise

1 Preheat the broiler. In a small bowl, stir together the brown sugar, lime juice, nutmeg, and allspice until smooth.

2 Spray a broiler pan with nonstick cooking spray. Place the bananas, cut-side up, on the broiler pan. Brush with half of the brown sugar mixture. Broil 4 to 6 inches from the heat for 3 minutes.

3 Brush with the remaining brown sugar mixture and broil until the bananas are soft and lightly colored, about 2 minutes. *Makes 4 servings*

Honey-Broiled Bananas Use 2 tablespoons honey in place of the brown sugar. Substitute lemon juice for the lime juice.

Orange-Currant Waffles

Soy protein powder often comes slightly sweetened and sometimes in flavors, such as vanilla or chocolate. Although this recipe was created with an unflavored soy protein powder, you could certainly use a vanilla-flavored one.

¾ cup all-purpose flour
¾ cup whole-wheat flour
½ cup unflavored soy protein powder
2 tablespoons sugar
1½ teaspoons baking powder
½ teaspoon baking soda
½ teaspoon salt
1 tablespoon grated orange zest
1½ cups buttermilk
3 tablespoons olive oil
⅔ cup dried currants
3 large egg whites

1 In a large bowl, combine the all-purpose flour, whole-wheat flour, soy protein powder, sugar, baking powder, baking soda, and salt. Stir in the orange zest.

2 In a medium bowl, combine the buttermilk and oil. Make a well in the center of the flour mixture and stir in the buttermilk mixture. Stir in the dried currants.

3 In a large bowl, beat the egg whites until stiff peaks form. Gently fold the beaten egg whites into the waffle batter.

4 Spray a nonstick waffle iron (with 4- to 4½-inch squares) with nonstick cooking spray. Preheat the iron. Spoon the batter into the iron, ½ cup per waffle, and cook until golden brown and crisp, about 2 minutes. Repeat with the remaining batter to make a total of 8 waffles. ***Makes 8 waffles***

per waffle	
calories	213
total fat	6g
saturated fat	1.1g
cholesterol	2mg
dietary fiber	3g
carbohydrate	32g
protein	9g
sodium	382mg

good source of:
riboflavin, selenium, thiamin

F.Y.I.

Compared with other legumes, soybeans are a complete source of protein since they have all essential amino acids required for the building and maintenance of human body tissues. Studies show that when substituted for animal protein in the diet, soy protein helps to reduce LDL cholesterol and triglycerides without having an adverse effect on the beneficial HDL cholesterol.

HOMEMADE

pancake mixes

Storebought pancakes mixes are usually made with lots of fat, and are certainly not designed with health in mind. These homemade pancake mixes are filled with extra healthful ingredients, including nonfat milk powder (for calcium) and soy protein powder. You can prepare multiple batches of these mixes and then store them in the freezer. Just take out what you need when you're in the mood to make pancakes. Each mix recipe makes 4 cups, and each cup of the mix will make 6 pancakes. So a full batch of pancake mix will make a total of 24 pancakes. **How to make pancakes:** To make 6 pancakes, measure out 1 cup of the mix and stir in one of the suggested mix-ins (*see below*). In a small bowl, stir together ¾ cup of water, 1 tablespoon of extra-light olive oil, and 1 large egg white. Stir the water mixture into the pancake mix until combined. Drop by ⅓ cupfuls onto a nonstick greased griddle or skillet and cook 1 minute per side, or until done.

- For the Indian Spiced Chick-Pea Pancakes, mix in 1 teaspoon grated lemon zest.

- For the Toasted Oat Pancakes, mix in ⅓ cup of raisins or chopped apricots.

- For the Chocolate Pancakes, mix in ⅓ cup of dried cherries.

Indian-Spiced Chick-Pea Pancake Mix

1¼ cups all-purpose flour

1 cup whole-wheat flour

1 cup chick-pea flour

⅔ cup nonfat dry milk powder

2 tablespoons sugar

2 tablespoons baking powder

1½ teaspoons salt

1 teaspoon cardamom

In a large bowl, stir together the all-purpose flour, whole-wheat flour, chick-pea flour, nonfat milk powder, sugar, baking powder, salt, and cardamom until well combined. *Makes 24 pancakes*

PER PANCAKE: 95 CALORIES, 2.6G TOTAL FAT (0.3G SATURATED), 0MG CHOLESTEROL, 1G DIETARY FIBER, 14G CARBOHYDRATE, 4G PROTEIN, 234MG SODIUM. **GOOD SOURCE OF:** RIBOFLAVIN, SELENIUM

Toasted Oat Pancake Mix

1 cup old-fashioned rolled oats

1⅓ cups whole-wheat flour

⅔ cup all-purpose flour

⅔ cup nonfat dry milk powder

¼ cup yellow cornmeal

2 tablespoons soy protein powder

2 tablespoons sugar

4 teaspoons baking powder

1 teaspoon salt

1 Preheat the oven to 400°F. Toast the oats until lightly browned, about 7 minutes. Transfer to a food processor and pulse until finely ground. Transfer to a bowl. 2 Stir in the whole-wheat flour, all-purpose flour, nonfat milk powder, cornmeal, soy protein powder, sugar, baking powder, and salt until well combined. *Makes 24 pancakes*

PER PANCAKE: 117 CALORIES, 2.7G TOTAL FAT (0.4G SATURATED), 0MG CHOLESTEROL, 2G DIETARY FIBER, 19G CARBOHYDRATE, 5G PROTEIN, 173MG SODIUM. **GOOD SOURCE OF:** RIBOFLAVIN, SELENIUM

Chocolate Pancake Mix

1¼ cups whole-wheat flour

1¼ cups all-purpose flour

¾ cup nonfat dry milk powder

½ cup wheat bran

⅓ cup soy protein powder

⅓ cup sugar

3 tablespoons unsweetened cocoa

3½ teaspoons baking powder

1 teaspoon baking soda

1 teaspoon salt

In a large bowl, stir together the whole-wheat flour, all-purpose flour, nonfat milk powder, wheat bran, soy protein powder, sugar, cocoa powder, baking powder, baking soda, and salt. *Makes 24 pancakes*

PER PANCAKE: 105 CALORIES, 2.6G TOTAL FAT (0.4G SATURATED), 0MG CHOLESTEROL, 2G DIETARY FIBER, 16G CARBOHYDRATE, 5G PROTEIN, 233MG SODIUM. **GOOD SOURCE OF:** RIBOFLAVIN, SELENIUM

Potato-Asparagus Frittata

A frittata is an Italian omelet. But unlike a traditional French-style omelet, the eggs are used more as a binder for the filling, with the proportion of egg to filling heavily weighted in favor of the vegetables. This makes a frittata fundamentally more healthful than a regular omelet, but we've made it even more so by using just egg whites.

1 pound small red potatoes, thinly sliced
¾ pound asparagus, cut into 1-inch lengths
⅓ cup water
1 tablespoon reduced-sodium soy sauce
1½ cups chopped red onion
1 tablespoon olive oil
10 large egg whites
½ teaspoon salt
½ teaspoon pepper

1 In a large pot of boiling water, cook the potatoes until tender, 7 to 10 minutes. Drain.

2 Meanwhile, in a vegetable steamer, cook the asparagus until crisp-tender, about 3 minutes.

3 In a 10-inch nonstick, broilerproof skillet, combine the water and soy sauce. Add the onion and cook until tender, about 5 minutes. Add the oil, potatoes, and asparagus to the pan.

4 In a large bowl, whisk together the egg whites, salt, and pepper. Pour the egg mixture over the vegetables and cook, without stirring, until the eggs are set around the edges and almost set in the center, about 15 minutes. Meanwhile, preheat the broiler.

5 Broil the frittata 4 to 6 inches from the heat for 1 to 2 minutes, or until the center is set. Cut into wedges to serve. ***Makes 4 servings***

ON THE *Menu*

This frittata is designed as a brunch dish, but it could just as easily be a vegetarian main course. Serve it with a salad of shredded romaine, chopped red onion, and diced red bell pepper tossed with a low-fat lemon vinaigrette. For dessert, try Pear-Cranberry Crumble (*page 133*).

Cinnamon-Apple Bran Muffins

To save a little time in the morning, you can put together all of the dry ingredients ahead of time. Combine all of the ingredients in step 2 and store them in a zip-seal bag in the freezer. When it's time to make the muffins, preheat the oven, prepare the muffin tins, and continue with step 3.

1½ cups flour
½ cup wheat bran
1 tablespoon baking powder
½ teaspoon salt
¾ teaspoon cinnamon
¼ teaspoon ground ginger
¼ teaspoon baking soda
1 cup buttermilk
½ cup packed dark brown sugar
3 tablespoons extra-light olive oil
1 large egg
Zest of 1 orange
1 cup diced unpeeled Granny Smith apple
1 tablespoon granulated sugar

1 Preheat the oven to 400°F. Line a 12-cup muffin tin with paper liners.

2 In a large bowl, combine the flour, bran, baking powder, salt, ½ teaspoon of the cinnamon, the ginger, and baking soda. Make a well in the center of the flour mixture.

3 In a medium bowl, whisk together the buttermilk, brown sugar, oil, egg, and orange zest. Pour the buttermilk mixture into the flour mixture, stirring until just combined. Fold in the apple. Do not overmix.

4 In a small bowl, stir together the granulated sugar and remaining ¼ teaspoon cinnamon.

5 Spoon the batter into the muffin cups. Sprinkle the cinnamon-sugar on top. Bake 12 to 15 minutes or until the muffins are golden and a toothpick inserted in the center comes out clean. *Makes 12 muffins*

Cinnamon-Pear Bran Muffins Substitute 1 cup diced Bartlett pear for the apple. Use lemon zest in place of orange zest.

F.Y.I.

Bran is the indigestible outer husk of wheat (as well as other cereal grains) and is one of the best sources of dietary fiber. Fiber plays a role in weight control by promoting a feeling of fullness.

Chocolate Swirl Quick Bread

Cinnamon provides a nice warm, spicy undertone to the chocolate in this tea bread.

<table>
<tr><td colspan="2">per slice</td></tr>
<tr><td>calories</td><td>227</td></tr>
<tr><td>total fat</td><td>4.6g</td></tr>
<tr><td>saturated fat</td><td>0.8g</td></tr>
<tr><td>cholesterol</td><td>1mg</td></tr>
<tr><td>dietary fiber</td><td>1g</td></tr>
<tr><td>carbohydrate</td><td>42g</td></tr>
<tr><td>protein</td><td>4g</td></tr>
<tr><td>sodium</td><td>256mg</td></tr>
</table>

good source of: riboflavin, selenium, thiamin

2 cups flour
¾ cup sugar
1½ teaspoons baking powder
½ teaspoon baking soda
½ teaspoon salt
2 large egg whites
3 tablespoons extra-light olive oil
1 cup buttermilk
1½ teaspoons vanilla extract
⅓ cup chocolate syrup
1 teaspoon cinnamon

1 Preheat the oven to 350°F. Spray a 9 x 5-inch loaf pan with nonstick cooking spray.

2 In a large bowl, stir together the flour, sugar, baking powder, baking soda, and salt. In a separate bowl, stir together the egg whites, oil, buttermilk, and vanilla. Make a well in the center of the flour mixture and stir in the buttermilk mixture until evenly moistened.

3 Scoop out ⅔ cup of the batter and transfer it to a medium bowl. Add the chocolate syrup and cinnamon and stir until combined.

4 Spoon the remaining batter into the loaf pan. Drop the chocolate batter onto the vanilla batter and, with a knife, swirl the chocolate batter through the vanilla batter.

5 Bake for 45 to 50 minutes, or until a toothpick inserted in the center comes out clean. Cool the loaf in the pan for 10 minutes, then invert onto the rack to cool completely. ***Makes 10 slices***

F.Y.I.

Olive oil that has little or no olive flavor is labeled "Light," "Extra-light," or "Mild-flavored," depending on the manufacturer. These olive oils are intentionally bland so that you can use them in recipes where you don't want the oil to add flavor, such as in muffins, quickbreads, or pancakes. The "light" on the label refers to flavor and not fat content, since all olive oils have the same number of calories and fat grams; all of them also have the same high level of heart-healthy monounsaturated fats.

Orange-Scented Zucchini Bread

Because zucchini has such a mild flavor, it adds texture and moisture to this tea bread without giving it a vegetable-y flavor.

1½ cups flour
⅔ cup sugar
2 teaspoons baking powder
½ teaspoon baking soda
½ teaspoon salt
1 teaspoon cardamom
½ teaspoon cinnamon
2 large egg whites
½ cup buttermilk
3 tablespoons extra-light olive oil
2 teaspoons grated orange zest
1½ cups shredded zucchini (about 2 medium)
⅓ cup raisins

1 Preheat the oven to 350°F. Spray a 9 x 5-inch loaf pan with nonstick cooking spray.

2 In a large bowl, stir together the flour, sugar, baking powder, baking soda, salt, cardamom, and cinnamon.

3 In a separate bowl, stir together the egg whites, buttermilk, oil, and orange zest. Stir in the zucchini.

4 Make a well in the center of the flour mixture and pour in the zucchini mixture. Stir just until evenly moistened. Fold in the raisins.

5 Pour the batter into the loaf pan and bake for 1 hour, or until a toothpick inserted in the center comes out clean. Cool in the pan on a rack for 10 minutes, then invert onto the rack to cool completely. ***Makes 10 slices***

Carrot-Apricot Bread Substitute shredded carrot for the zucchini, and use diced dried apricots instead of raisins.

F.Y.I.

Cinnamon is the dried inner bark of a tropical evergreen tree, of which there are about 100 different species, all with similar aromatic properties. The two most commonly available varieties are Ceylonese cinnamon and Chinese cinnamon. Chinese cinnamon, which is actually from the bark of the cassia tree, is not considered a true cinnamon (species *Cinnamomum verum*). Grown in Southern China and other parts of East Asia, cassia is a dark reddish color and stronger in flavor than its Ceylonese cousin (*Cinnamomum zeylancium*). Cassia is less expensive to process than true cinnamons and is the type of "cinnamon" most commonly sold in supermarkets—though it is sometimes blended with Ceylonese cinnamon.

Spotlite recipe

Pumpkin Seed Granola

5 cups old-fashioned rolled oats
¾ cup hulled pumpkin seeds
½ cup toasted wheat germ
½ cup maple syrup
¼ cup frozen apple juice concentrate
⅓ cup packed light brown sugar
2 tablespoons extra-light olive oil
1 teaspoon vanilla extract
½ teaspoon salt
2 cups dried cherries or dried cranberries

1 Preheat the oven to 300°F. Spray a baking pan with nonstick cooking spray. In a large bowl, toss together the oats, pumpkin seeds, and wheat germ. Transfer the mixture to the baking sheet and bake until lightly crisped and browned, about 30 minutes.

2 Meanwhile, in a small saucepan, combine the maple syrup, apple juice concentrate, brown sugar, and oil. Stir over medium heat until the brown sugar has dissolved, about 2 minutes. Remove from the heat and stir in the vanilla and salt.

3 After the oat mixture has baked 30 minutes, pour the maple mixture over the oat mixture and stir well to coat. Increase the oven temperature to 350°F. Return the granola to the oven and bake until no longer wet, about 20 minutes.

4 Break up the clumps of granola with a spoon and let cool to room temperature. Transfer the mixture to a large bowl, add the cherries, and toss to combine. Store in an airtight container. ***Makes 8 cups***

PER ⅓ CUP **212 calories, 5.5g total fat (1g saturated), 0mg cholesterol, 4g dietary fiber, 34g carbohydrate, 7g protein, 95mg sodium**
Good source of: **magnesium, thiamin, zinc**

Although there are lots of commercial granolas available, they are all quite high in fat. This homemade granola is low in fat, and the fat it does contain is primarily healthful mono-unsaturated fat. The roasted pumpkin seeds in the granola are packed with fiber and minerals as well as alpha-linolenic acid, a type of fat that may help prevent hardening of the arteries. You'll also benefit from the rolled oats, which are a top source of cholesterol-lowering soluble fiber. And regardless of which type of dried fruit you use, it will supply important nutrients and fiber, as well as some potentially healthful phytochemicals.

THE SAVVY SHOPPER

all-fruit spread There does not seem to be any consistency in labeling for fruit spreads: they can be called various things, including all-fruit, spreadable fruit, or 100% fruit. But underneath it all they are all "jams" that are made with nothing but fruit and fruit juice and have no refined sugar. They are slightly lower in calories and carbohydrates than regular jam: 1 tablespoon of regular jam has about 50 calories and 13 grams of sugars; 1 tablespoon of all-fruit spread has 40 calories and about 8 grams of sugars.

allspice Allspice is a dark, round, dried berry about the size of a large peppercorn and is available as whole berries or ground. Allspice tastes like a blend of spices (cloves, cinnamon, and nutmeg), and many people mistakenly take its name to mean that it is, in fact, a blend. Like black pepper, allspice has the most flavor if freshly ground when you use it.

apple butter Apple butter is applesauce that has been cooked down until it achieves the thickness of a jam; it often has some spices, such as cinnamon and allspice added to it, too. The natural pectin content of apples gives apple butter a jamlike consistency without the addition of the huge amounts of sugar ordinarily required in jam making. The pectin content of apple butter also makes it a good substitute for some of the fat called for in simple baking recipes, such as brownies.

beans, canned Many types of beans—black beans, red kidney beans, cannellini (white kidney beans), chick-peas, pinto beans—are available in canned form. They are a great and convenient source of low-fat protein, complex carbohydrates, soluble fiber, and the B vitamin folate. The only downside to them is their sodium content. However, if you place the beans in a strainer and run cold water over them to rinse off the liquid they come packed in, you will reduce the sodium content considerably. This also removes some of the water-soluble B vitamins, but it's a fair trade. Keep canned beans in your pantry, but consider cooking your own beans from scratch and then freezing them so you can use them at a moment's notice.

bulgur Bulgur is cracked wheat that undergoes a process similar to that used for converted rice: The whole-wheat kernels are steam-cooked and dried. Bulgur is then cracked into three different granulations. Traditionally, the coarsest grain is used for pilaf; the medium, for cereal; and the finest, for salads such as tabbouleh. Supermarket bulgur may not specify granulation and is probably a medium-grain so that it can be used in a number of different ways. Fine-grained bulgur can also be "cooked" by soaking, without heat.

buttermilk Buttermilk is a milk product made by adding a special bacterial culture to fat-free or low-fat milk. Buttermilk lends a tangy taste, a slightly thickened texture, and a subtle richness to soups, stews, casseroles, and sauces. But one of its most important uses is in baked goods. Buttermilk's acidity inhibits the development of gluten (a tough protein in flour), so baked goods made with buttermilk turn out tender but without much fat. For baking, if you don't have buttermilk, you can make your own "soured" milk: To make 1 cup of soured milk, place 1 tablespoon lemon juice or vinegar in a cup measure. Add enough low-fat (1%) milk to measure 1 cup.

cheese, feta Feta cheese is a soft, crumbly, cured Greek cheese, traditionally made from sheep's or goat's milk. Chalk-white and rindless, feta is usually available as rectangular blocks packed in brine; it's best to rinse it before using to eliminate some of the sodium. Because feta is so highly flavorful, a little goes a long way.

cilantro Mexican and Indian food would not be the same without cilantro, also called coriander leaf or Chinese parsley. The leaves, which resembles those of flat-leaf parsley (and are in the same botanical family) are strongly aromatic. Cilantro's distinctive flavor is not to everyone's taste—in fact, some researchers believe that there is a genetic component to an individual's reaction to cilantro. If a recipe calls for cilantro and you can't find any fresh, don't bother buying dried cilantro; it has no flavor whatsoever. In fact, you'd be better off substituting fresh basil instead.

cocoa powder, unsweetened Unsweetened cocoa powder is powdered pure chocolate with most of the fat removed. Most supermarket brands of cocoa powder have about 0.5 grams of fat and 20 calories per tablespoon (which is about 10% fat by volume, and 25% of its calories from fat). Cocoa does have some nutritional value, including minerals and phytochemicals. Cocoa

powder labeled "Dutch-process" has been treated with an alkali to neutralize some of the acid to create a milder flavor. Although most people think of cocoa for making hot drinks or as a baking ingredient, it is actually good in a variety of savory dishes, such as soups, stews, or barbecue sauces. Add a tablespoon or so to your next pot of homemade chili to temper and meld the spices and to slightly thicken the sauce.

currants Currants are tiny raisins dried from a small variety of grape called Corinth grapes (hence the name currants, which is a distortion of Corinth). In their fresh form, Corinth grapes are often sold in the market as "champagne grapes," because their tiny clusters supposedly resemble champagne bubbles. You can use currants interchangeably with raisins, keeping in mind that currants are smaller and will disperse more flavor and sweetness because you get more currants in every bite.

flour, cake Cake flour is milled from soft wheat, which is lower in gluten than hard wheat. Gluten is a protein that toughens when kneaded and cooked, making it a desirable component of such things as

bread and pasta, where a sturdy structure is required. In cakes, however, less gluten is preferable in order to give the cake a fine-textured, tender crumb. (By the way, cake flour is not to be confused with self-rising flour, which is flour that has had leavening agents added to it.) If you need to substitute regular all-purpose flour for cake flour, place 2 tablespoons cornstarch in a 1-cup dry measure and spoon in enough all-purpose flour to measure 1 level cup.

ginger, crystallized Crystallized ginger is fresh ginger that has been coarsely chopped and cooked in a sugar syrup to "candy" it. The candied ginger is then coated in sugar to give it a rough, crunchy surface. Sweet-hot in flavor, crystallized ginger is used in baking, as a garnish for desserts, and in spicy condiments and sauces. Look for it in the spice section of the supermarket or in bulk at candy stores, gourmet shops, and Asian groceries (it's usually much cheaper when purchased in bulk).

green chilies, canned Canned green chilies tend to be either pickled green jalapeños or those simply labeled "mild." Use the mild green chilies—which come whole or chopped—to add a subtly piquant green chili flavor to dishes. Because the chilies are packed in brine, it's usually wise to drain them to reduce the amount of sodium that ends up in the dish.

honey Honey is a convenient sweetener, especially in cold dishes, because you don't have to dissolve sugar over heat: The honeybee has already processed it for you. While insignificant in nutrients other than calories, honey can be found in assorted flavors (depending on where the bees gathered the nectar), styles, and colors. Honey should never be given to infants under 1 year as they lack certain stomach acids that would protect them against certain strains of botulin toxins, which may be present in honey. When measuring out honey, pour it into a measuring cup or spoon that has been sprayed with nonfat cooking spray as this prevents the honey from sticking to the utensil.

mandarin oranges Mandarins are a class of orange with loose, easily peeled "zipper" skin and segments that separate more easily than those of regular oranges. Mandarins and tangerines are similar and in some cases the terms are used interchangeably. Native to China, mandarins (in cans) have made their way onto American supermarkets shelves as an ingredient for Chinese-style dishes. Although the canned mandarins have lost some of their vitamin C in the processing, they are convenient to have on hand for adding to salads and desserts.

maple sugar This is maple syrup with all the liquid evaporated, leaving behind a dry sugar. It comes both in pressed cakes and in a granulated form. Except for the fact that it is very expensive, this is a good substitute for refined sugar because the mouth perceives it as much sweeter than white sugar and you can use less of it.

maple syrup Maple syrup is the boiled sap of the sugar maple tree and is produced primarily in New England and eastern Canada. (The reason for this is apparently a combination of the climate, the angle of sunlight, and the soil.) Maple syrup is available in several grades (though the commonest is Grade A) and they are all fairly expensive, partly because of the labor-intensive process involved in making maple syrup. Although there are imitation syrups available, they lack the inimitable sweetness of the real thing (they are also a bit higher in calories).

mayonnaise Like many other high-fat foods, mayonnaise comes in several versions that have less fat than the standard product. For our recipes we have chosen to use the reduced-fat version (usually labeled "Light"), because although the fat-free and low-fat versions have less fat, they taste oddly sweet.

milk, dry To make nonfat dry milk powder, liquid milk has some of its water partially evaporated. Then this slightly condensed milk is sprayed in a drying chamber to dehydrate it. The resulting powder is reconstituted by adding water (usually about 1 cup of water to 3 tablespoons of milk powder). Use nonfat dry milk to boost the calcium and protein content of recipes or even of liquid milk. A tablespoon of nonfat dry milk contains 94 milligrams of calcium, 27 calories, and no fat, and has added vitamins A and D.

milk, evaporated Evaporated milk is homogenized milk that has had much of its water removed, leaving behind a concentration of milk fat and solids. It has a slightly sweet taste because of the concentration of lactose (milk sugar), but it should not be confused with sweetened condensed milk, which has sugar added to it. Evaporated milk comes in a number of forms, depending on how much of the milk fat has been removed. There are regular (full-fat), low-fat (2%), and fat-free forms. Store at room temperature for up to 6 months until opened, then refrigerate for up to 1 week.

mint The type of mint most commonly found in supermarkets is spearmint (also called garden mint). Generally only the mint leaves are used. The stems are perfectly edible, but don't have much flavor. Mint in its dried form is a reasonable substitute for the fresh.

oats Oats are a wonderful addition to the health-conscious cook's pantry. Not only do they have lots of protein, they are also very high in soluble fiber, which has been credited with helping to lower blood cholesterol levels. In the late 1990s, the FDA allowed the labels on oat products the bear the statement that soluble fiber, when a part of a diet low in saturated fat and cholesterol, "may reduce the risk of heart disease." The most familiar form of oats is the old-fashioned rolled oats, formed when whole oat grains (called groats) are heated and pressed

flat with steel rollers. There are also quick-cooking oats—the oats are sliced before being rolled—and instant oatmeal, precooked, dried groats rolled very thin. All of these products have soluble fiber, though what a recipe calls for will depend on the texture that the dish requires. Naturally, the whole rolled oats have more texture than the instant oats.

oil, dark sesame The sesame oil most commonly found in supermarkets is a dark, polyunsaturated oil, pressed from toasted sesame seeds. Since it is often used in Asian cuisines, and because many brands of this oil have Asian-sounding names, cookbooks often refer to it as "Asian sesame oil," but in the store you will not find any labels that say this. The label may say "sesame oil" or sometimes "roasted sesame oil." You will also find cold-pressed sesame oil in health-food stores; this type of oil is not from toasted sesame seeds, and is light in both flavor and color. The dark oil breaks down when heated, so it is not used for sautéing, but rather as a seasoning, added at the end of cooking.

olives, calamata Calamata olives are ripe, purple-black, brine-cured Greek olives that

add a distinctive bite to salads, pasta sauces, and other savory dishes. They are often sold packed in vinegar and are a familiar supermarket olive. One of their distinct culinary virtues is that they are easy to pit. Use sparingly as Calamatas (like all olives) naturally contain fat, and the curing process adds considerable salt.

onions, pearl These tiny onions are so densely planted that they attain a size of only an inch or less in diameter. While pearl onions were once only available as white onions, they are now available in white, gold, and dark red or purple varieties. They are the onion of choice in certain stews (coq au vin is the classic example), soups, and sautés. However, they can be a bit of a chore to prepare, so frozen already-peeled pearl onions are a convenient substitute for fresh.

onions, vidalia Vidalias are "sweet" onions, one of a number of such types grown primarily from fall to spring in warm-weather states, such as Georgia, which is where Vidalias come from (they are named for the town of Vidalia). Sweet onions have a very high water and sugar content, which means that they spoil more quickly and do not hold up as well as other onions. Other examples of sweet onions are OSO Sweet, Texas Sweet, Walla Walla, Maui, and Amerisweet.

parsnips Parsnips are an old-fashioned vegetable that deserve more attention. These pale yellow to off-white roots are a member of the *Umbelliferae* family, whose members include carrots, celery, chervil, fennel, and parsley. Parsnips are planted in the spring and are then left in the ground until a hard frost occurs in late fall, which causes the starches in the vegetable to convert to sugars, giving the roots their pleasantly sweet, nutty flavor. In fact, parsnips are one of the few vegetables that actually benefits from an early frost. Although they can grow up to 20 inches in length, they are most tender when about 8 inches long—roughly the size of a large carrot.

pectin Pectin is a soluble fiber (found in the peel of many fruits) that when heated turns into a gel. This property of pectin is what gives jams and jellies their texture. Although some fruits have enough natural pectin to "set up" on their own, many low-pectin fruits require a boost so that the resulting jam will be firm. To compensate for low-pectin fruits, home canners can buy commercial pectin, which comes in liquid or powdered form, to add to their jams and jellies. Most commercial pectins are made from ground up citrus peels processed to extract the pectin. Some commercial pectins also have an acid or sweet component (both of which help to set the jam).

peppers, jalapeño
Jalapeño peppers are hot green chili peppers about two inches long and an inch in diameter, with rounded tips. Most of the heat resides in the membranes (ribs) of the pepper, so remove them for a milder effect—wear gloves to protect your hands from the volatile oils. Jalapeños are also sold pickled, whole or sliced. Although a really good fresh jalapeño has an incomparable flavor, there can be a wide range of heat; sometimes you'll get a fresh chili that has no more heat than a green bell pepper. Pickled jalapeños, on the other hand, are a reliable source of chili heat.

potatoes, baking In the supermarket, potatoes are likely to be labeled according to their end use: baking potatoes, for example, are low in moisture and high in starch, with a so-called "mealy" flesh. Their starchy flesh gets fluffier than other potatoes when baked or mashed. On the other hand, they are not well suited for potato salad, because if you cut them into chunks before cooking them, they will not hold their shape (whereas waxy "boiling" potatoes will).

pumpkin, canned Canned pumpkin, often labeled "solid-pack pumpkin," is an unsweetened puree of cooked pumpkin (and not to be confused with canned pumpkin pie filling, which has added sugar and spices). It is a convenience for cooks who do not have hours to spend cooking fresh pumpkin down to a thick concentrate. Although most people have probably used pumpkin puree to make pies, this wonderfully nutritious ingredient (extremely high in beta carotene) can also be used in soups, quick breads, cakes, and sauces.

rice, aromatic "Aromatic" is an umbrella term for rices that have a toasty, nutty fragrance and a flavor reminiscent of popcorn or roasted nuts. They are primarily long-grain varieties. Perhaps the best-known aromatic rice is basmati grown in India. It has a nutlike fragrance while cooking and a delicate, almost buttery flavor. There are also a number of basmati-like aromatic rices that have been developed in this country and that are sold under trade names, including: Jasmati, Kasmati, and Texmati.

sherry Sherry is a fortified wine originally made in Spain but now produced elsewhere as well. Sherries range in sweetness from quite dry (labeled fino, manzanillo, or simply "dry") to medium-dry (labeled amontillado or "milk sherry") to sweet (oloroso, also called "cream" or "golden"). Use a dry sherry to add a fragrant bouquet to savory sauces.

soy protein powder Soy protein powder is made from defatted soy flakes and is most often sold mixed with other ingredients to make a product that can either be added to drinks or made into a drink itself. The added ingredients often include sugar and flavorings, such as vanilla. Soy protein powder is an especially good source of protein when compared with other soyfoods. Depending on the brand, one serving (about 2 heaping tablespoons) of soy protein powder can have 20 to 28 grams of protein. By contrast, a 4-ounce serving of firm tofu has about 18 grams of protein and an 8-ounce glass of soymilk has only 6 grams of protein.

split peas Split peas are one of the more satisfying dried legumes available to the cook. Unlike beans such as kidney beans, split peas do not need to be presoaked, and they take only about 45 minutes to cook. They are very low in fat and rich in B vitamins and iron. Green split peas are the commonest, but yellow split peas are available too.

tomatoes, sun-dried Sun-dried tomatoes are plum tomatoes that have been dried slowly to produce a chewy, intensely flavorful ingredient. Choose the dry-packed type, since the oil-packed type are higher in fat and often contain seasonings that may not work in the dish you are preparing. If the sun-dried tomatoes you get are very soft, you can use them as is, but often the tomatoes must be soaked in hot water to soften them. And if the recipe calls for using the tomato-soaking liquid, follow the instructions even if the tomatoes are soft.

vinegar, balsamic Often mistaken for a wine vinegar, balsamic vinegar is actually made from highly concentrated grape juice (usually from the white Trebbiano grape) that never becomes wine, but is reduced by cooking and then aged in wooden barrels. Authentic balsamic vinegar from Italy comes in both commercially-made (*industriale*) and traditionally-made (*tradizionale*) forms. The commercially made is manufactured in bulk and may or may not be aged. This is the type found most commonly in supermarkets. Traditional balsamic carries a much heftier price tag, because it is always aged. Because this vinegar is so mild, you can make dressings and marinades using less oil.

watercress Watercress is a member of the *Cruciferae* (mustard) family, which also includes broccoli, kale, and mustard greens. It has small, crisp, dark green leaves and a peppery, slightly bitter flavor. It's a wonderful addition to salads and has a good amount of vitamin C, as well as some beta carotene.

zest, citrus Citrus zest is the thin, outermost colored part of the rind of citrus fruits that contains strongly flavored oils. Zest imparts an intense flavor that makes a refreshing contrast to the richness of meat, poultry, or fish. Remove the zest with a grater, citrus zester, or vegetable peeler; be careful to remove only the colored layer, not the spongy white pith beneath it.

Leading Sources of

fiber

food	calories	fiber (g)
†Black beans, cooked, 1 cup	227	15
†Chick-peas, cooked, 1 cup	269	12.5
†Baby lima beans, cooked, 1 cup	189	10.8
†Green peas, cooked, 1 cup	134	8.8
Raspberries, 1 cup	60	8.4
Bulgur, cooked, 1 cup	151	8.2
Blackberries, 1 cup	75	7.6
†Baked sweet potato, with skin, 8 oz	279	7.3
†Oat bran, ½ cup	116	7.2
†Dried figs, 3 medium	145	7.0
Dried pears, ½ cup	236	6.8
Artichoke, 1 medium	60	6.5
Whole-wheat pasta, cooked, 1 cup	174	6.3
Wheat bran, ¼ cup	31	6.2
†Dried plums (prunes), ½ cup	203	6.0
†Barley, cooked, 1 cup	193	6.0
†Dried apricots, ½ cup	155	5.9
Butternut squash, cooked, 1 cup	82	5.7
Baked potato, with skin, 8 oz	247	5.4
†Carrots, cooked, 1 cup	70	5.1
Buckwheat groats, cooked, 1 cup	155	4.5
†Hass avocado, ½ medium	153	4.2
Pear, 1 fresh	98	4.0
†Oatmeal, cooked, 1 cup	145	4.0
Blueberries, 1 cup	81	3.9
Almonds, roasted, 1 oz	166	3.9
Sunflower seeds, ¼ cup	205	3.8
†Apple, with skin, 1 medium	81	3.7
Wheat germ, toasted, ¼ cup	108	3.6
Brown rice, cooked, 1 cup	216	3.5
Strawberries, 1 cup	43	3.3
†Carrots, 1 cup grated raw	47	3.3
Mushrooms, cooked, 1 cup	48	2.4
Grapefruit, ½ medium	39	1.3

†Foods particularly high in soluble fiber.

low-fat protein

food	protein (g)	fat (g)
Beef top round, cooked, 3 oz	30	6.0
Pork loin, cooked, 3 oz	26	5.7
Chicken breast*, cooked, 3 oz	26	3.0
Turkey breast*, cooked, 3 oz	26	0.6
Beef bottom round, cooked, 3 oz	24	6.3
Turkey dark meat*, cooked, 3 oz	24	6.1
Pork tenderloin, cooked, 3 oz	24	4.1
Duck breast*, cooked, 3 oz	23	2.1
Flank steak, cooked, 3 oz	23	8.6
TVP, ¾ cup dry	23	0.4
Snapper, cooked, 3 oz	22	1.5
Chicken thigh*, cooked, 3 oz	22	9.3
Salmon, cooked, 3 oz	22	6.9
Tempeh, 4 oz	22	8.7
Soybeans, cooked, ¾ cup	21	12
Sole/flounder, cooked, 3 oz	21	1.3
Tuna, water-packed, 3 oz	20	2.5
Lentils, cooked, 1 cup	18	0.8
Scallops, cooked, 3 oz	18	3.4
Shrimp, cooked, 3 oz	18	0.9
Kidney beans, cooked, 1 cup	15	0.9
Black beans, cooked, 1 cup	15	0.6
Chick peas, cooked, 1 cup	15	4.2
Low-fat yogurt, 1 cup	13	3.8
Baby lima beans, cooked, 1 cup	12	0.5
Egg whites, 3	11	0
Lite silken tofu, extra-firm, 4 oz	8	0.8

*skinless, boneless

Recommended Intakes

The charts below provide the adult RDAs established by the National Academy of Sciences for vitamins and minerals. For some vitamins and minerals, not enough is known to recommend a specific amount; in these cases, the Academy has recommended a range called the Estimated Safe and Adequate Daily Dietary Intake. All values are for adults (over age 19).

vitamins

Vitamin A	
women	700 mcg
men	900 mcg
Vitamin C	
women	75 mg
men	90 mg
Vitamin D	
age 19-50	200 IU
age 51-70	400 IU
age 70+	600 IU
Vitamin E	15 mg
Vitamin K	
women	90 mcg
men	120 mcg
Thiamin	
women	1.1 mg
men	1.2 mg
Riboflavin	
women	1.1 mg
men	1.3 mg
Niacin	
women	14 mg
men	16 mg
Pantothenic acid	5 mg
Vitamin B$_6$	
women and men 19-50	1.3 mg
women 51+	1.5 mg
men 51+	1.7 mg
Vitamin B$_{12}$	2.4 mcg
Folate (folic acid)	400 mcg
Biotin	30 mcg

minerals

Calcium	
age 19-50	1,000 mg
age 51+	1,200 mg
Chloride	No RDA
Chromium	
women 19-50	25 mcg
women 51+	20 mcg
men 19-50	35 mcg
men 51+	30 mcg
Copper	900 mcg
Fluoride	
women	3 mg
men	4 mg
Iodine	150 mcg
Iron	
women 19-50	18 mg
women 51+	8 mg
men 19+	8 mg
Magnesium	
women 19-30	310 mg
women 31+	320 mg
men 19-30	400 mg
men 31+	420 mg
Manganese	
women	1.8 mg
men	2.3 mg
Molybdenum	45 mcg
Phosphorus	700 mg
Potassium	1,600 to 2,000 mg minimum
Selenium	55 mcg
Sodium	2,400 mg maximum
Zinc	
women	8 mg
men	11 mg

recipe index

A

Appetizers
  Chili-Lime Corn Chips, 17
  Lemon-Curry Corn Chips, 17
  Mexican-Style Grilled Shrimp
    Cocktail, 16
  Spicy Pea Guacamole, 18
Apple-Glazed Pork Tenderloin, 59
Apples
  Apple-Winter Squash Soup, 26
  Cabbage & Apple Slaw, 120
  Carrot, Apple & Ginger Shake, 108
  Grape & Raspberry-Poached Apples,
    128
  Rosemary & Orange-Scented Apples,
    128
Apricots
  Mango & Dried Fruit Compote, 124
Asian Barbecued Chicken Salad, 67
Asian Noodle Salad, 83
Asparagus
  Bulgur with Asparagus & Peas, 115
  Grilled Vegetable Salad, 95
  Pasta with Asparagus & Snow Peas,
    111
  Potato-Asparagus Frittata, 141
  Sesame Asparagus & Snow Peas, 111

B

Baked Butternut Squash, 101
Baked Pinto Beans, 104
Balsamic Vinaigrette, Fat-Free, 119
Bananas
  Banana-Kiwi Salsa, 69
  Breakfast Fruit Salad, 137
  Brown Sugar-Broiled Bananas, 138
  Honey-Broiled Bananas, 138
Barbecued Chicken Salad, 67
Barley
  Carrot & Barley Soup with Basil, 20
  Mushroom, Root Vegetable & Barley
    Soup, 27
  Shrimp & Barley Salad with Lemon-
    Cilantro Dressing, 42
Bass (saltwater)
  Oven-Steamed Bass with Thai-Style
    Vegetables, 31
  Striped Bass Provençale, 44

Beans, dried or canned. *See also Chick-*
  peas
  Baked Pinto Beans, 104
  Bean & Butternut Chili, 96
  Louisiana Rice & Bean Salad, 86
  Pasta with White Beans, Carrots &
    Tomatoes, 85
  Red Bean, Rice & Shrimp Salad, 86
  Roasted Pepper & Black Bean Soup, 24
  Rutabaga & Black Bean Couscous, 92
  Tomato & Cannellini Salad with
    Roasted Garlic Dressing, 121
  Tomato-Bean Salad with Orzo, 121
Beef
  Classic Fajitas, 54
  Pot Roast with Winter Vegetables, 58
  Soy & Ginger Braised Beef, 52
  Unstuffed Peppers, 56
Berry Cheesecake Mousse, 131
Beverages. *See Shakes*
Bisque, Tomato-Shrimp, 30
Black beans
  Roasted Pepper & Black Bean
    Soup, 24
  Rutabaga & Black Bean Couscous, 92
Blueberries
  Berry Cheesecake Mousse, 131
  Hot Berry Sundaes, 123
Bok choy
  Capellini with Barbecued Pork &
    Vegetables, 57
Braised Pork & Root Vegetables, 52
Bran
  Cinnamon-Apple Bran Muffins, 142
  Cinnamon-Pear Bran Muffins, 142
Bread Pudding, Cinnamon-Raisin, 127
Bread Salad, Italian, with Mozzarella &
  Roasted Peppers, 99
Bread. *See also Muffins*
  Carrot-Apricot Bread, 144
  Chocolate Swirl Quick Bread, 143
  Orange-Scented Zucchini Bread, 144
Breakfast/brunch
  Breakfast Fruit Salad, 137
  Brown Sugar-Broiled Bananas, 138
  Chocolate Pancake Mix, 140
  Cinnamon-Apple Bran Muffins, 142
  Honey-Broiled Bananas, 138
  Indian-Spiced Chick-Pea Pancake
    Mix, 140

  Orange-Currant Waffles, 139
  Potato-Asparagus Frittata, 141
  Pumpkin Seed Granola, 145
Broccoli
  Brown Rice Pasta with Broccoli &
    Sun-Dried Tomatoes, 82
  Chicken, Broccoli & Tomato Stir-Fry,
    78
  Cremini, Broccoli & Corn Salad, 98
Broiled Chicken with Spicy Lemon-
  Carrot Sauce, 74
Broth
  Chicken Broth, 25
  Green Herb Broth, 25
  Onion Broth, 25
Brown Rice Pasta with Broccoli & Sun-
  Dried Tomatoes, 82
Brown Sugar-Broiled Bananas, 138
Brownies, Cocoa, 129
Buckwheat. *See Kasha*
Bulgur
  Bulgur with Asparagus & Peas, 115
  Lemony Bulgur & Shrimp Salad, 49
Burgers
  Dilled Tuna Burger, 47
  Mexican-Style Turkey Burgers, 68
  Portobello Cheeseburgers, 94
  Thai Tuna Burger, 47
  Veggie Burgers, 84
Buttermilk, Indian-Spiced, 108
Butternut squash
  Baked Butternut Squash, 101
  Bean & Butternut Chili, 96
  Rice-Stuffed Butternut Squash, 101

C

Cabbage
  Cabbage & Apple Slaw, 120
  Coleslaw, 120
  Sweet & Sour Red Cabbage, 106
Cake, Strawberry Long, 125
Cantaloupe
  Breakfast Fruit Salad, 137
Capellini with Barbecued Pork &
  Vegetables, 57
Carrots
  Braised Pork & Root Vegetables, 52
  Carrot, Apple & Ginger Shake, 108
  Carrot & Barley Soup with Basil, 20
  Carrot-Apricot Bread, 144

Creamy Carrot & Rice Soup, 20
Pasta with White Beans, Carrots &
Tomatoes, 85
Soy & Ginger Braised Beef, 52
Cereal
Pumpkin Seed Granola, 145
Cheesecake
Berry Cheesecake Mousse, 131
Pumpkin Cheesecake Puddings, 134
Cherries
Breakfast Fruit Salad, 137
One-Crust Sour Cherry Pie, 136
Quinoa with Peanuts & Dried
Cherries, 117
Chick-peas
Chick-Pea & Pesto Pizza, 89
Winter Vegetable Couscous, 92
Yellow Pepper & Chick-Pea Soup, 24
Chicken. *See also Game hens*
Asian Barbecued Chicken Salad, 67
Barbecued Chicken Salad, 67
Broiled Chicken with Spicy Lemon-
Carrot Sauce, 74
Chicken, Broccoli & Tomato Stir-Fry,
78
Chicken Broth, 25
Chicken Curry with Wide Noodles, 66
Chicken in Shiitake-Tomato
Sauce, 76
Chicken-Onion Soup, 63
Coq au Vin Blanc, 79
Feta-Topped Baked Chicken &
Vegetables, 62
Greek-Style Chicken Salad, 62
Jamaican Jerked Chicken, 61
Onion-Chicken Fajitas, 70
Pasta with Hunter-Style Chicken, 72
Provençal Chicken Stew, 71
Chili, Bean & Butternut, 96
Chili-Broiled Snapper, 50
Chili-Lime Corn Chips, 17
Chips
Chili-Lime Corn Chips, 17
Lemon-Curry Corn Chips, 17
Chocolate Pancake Mix, 140
Chocolate Swirl Quick Bread, 143
Chowder
Spicy Clam Chowder, 51
Spicy Shrimp Chowder, 51
Tomato-Vegetable Chowder, 21

Cilantro Rice with Ham & Corn, 114
Cinnamon-Apple Bran Muffins, 142
Cinnamon-Pear Bran Muffins, 142
Cinnamon-Raisin Bread Pudding, 127
Citrus Salsa, 69
Clam Chowder, Spicy, 51
Classic Fajitas, 54
Cocoa Brownies, 129
Codfish
Cod en Papillote, 40
Fish Stew Arrabbiata, 45
Potato Pasta with Tomatoes, Peppers
& Cod, 39
Coleslaw, 120
Cookies
Cocoa Brownies, 129
Coq au Vin Blanc, 79
Corn
Chili Corn Pudding, 103
Cilantro Rice with Ham & Corn, 114
Corn Pudding with Roasted Peppers &
Scallions, 103
Corn Salsa, 69
Cremini, Broccoli & Corn Salad, 98
Cornmeal
Polenta with Meatless Mushroom
Sauce, 97
Couscous
Rutabaga & Black Bean Couscous, 92
Winter Vegetable Couscous, 92
Cranberries
Cranberry-Ginger Hens, 64
Individual Pumpkin Soufflés, 126
Maple Sweet Potatoes with
Cranberries, 105
Pear-Cranberry Crumble, 133
Pumpkin Seed Granola, 145
Creamy Carrot & Rice Soup, 20
Cremini, Broccoli & Corn Salad, 98
Crumble, Pear-Cranberry, 133
Cucumber, Yogurt-, Shake, 108
Currant-Glazed Pork Tenderloin, 59
Curry/curried food
Chicken Curry with Wide Noodles, 66
Curried Split Pea & Mushroom Soup,
28
Curry-Broiled Snapper, 50
Shrimp & Sweet Potato Curry, 38

D
Desserts
Berry Cheesecake Mousse, 131
Breakfast Fruit Salad, 137
Brown Sugar-Broiled Bananas, 138
Cinnamon-Raisin Bread Pudding, 127
Cocoa Brownies, 129
Fresh Fruit Gelatin, 132
Grape & Raspberry-Poached Apples,
128
Grilled Pineapple with Maple Cream,
135
Honey-Broiled Bananas, 138
Hot Berry Sundaes, 123
Individual Pumpkin Soufflés, 126
Mango & Dried Fruit Compote, 124
One-Crust Sour Cherry Pie, 136
Pear-Cranberry Crumble, 133
Pumpkin Cheesecake Puddings, 134
Rosemary & Orange-Scented Apples,
128
Strawberry Long Cake, 125
Winter Fruit Gratin, 130
Dilled Tuna Burger, 47
Dressing. *See Salad dressing*
Dutch Lettuce, Vegetarian, 112

E-F
Eggplant
Penne with Ratatouille Sauce, 90
Eggs
Potato-Asparagus Frittata, 141
Fajitas
Classic Fajitas, 54
Onion-Chicken Fajitas, 70
Fat-Free Balsamic Vinaigrette, 119
Fat-Free Pineapple-Tarragon Dressing,
119
Feta-Topped Baked Chicken &
Vegetables, 62
Fettuccine & Sugar Snaps with Almond-
Orange Pesto, 88
Fish. *See also specific types*
Baked Flounder with Two Tomatoes,
37
Chili-Broiled Snapper, 50
Cinnamon-Pear Bran Muffins, 142
Cod en Papillote, 40
Curry-Broiled Snapper, 50

recipe index

Fish *continued*
- Dilled Tuna Burger, 47
- Fish Stew Arrabbiata, 45
- Italian-Style Monkfish Stir-Fry, 32
- Oven-Steamed Bass with Thai-Style Vegetables, 31
- Potato Pasta with Tomatoes, Peppers & Cod, 39
- Spinach-Stuffed Sole, 41
- Striped Bass Provençale, 44
- Swordfish Milanese, 43
- Thai Tuna Burger, 47
- Vegetable-Topped Baked Haddock, 33

Flounder. *See also Sole*
- Baked Flounder with Two Tomatoes, 37

Fresh Fruit Gelatin, 132

Frittata, Potato-Asparagus, 141

Fruit. *See also specific types*
- Breakfast Fruit Salad, 137
- Brown Sugar-Broiled Bananas, 138
- Fresh Fruit Gelatin, 132
- Grape & Raspberry-Poached Apples, 128
- Grilled Pineapple with Maple Cream, 135
- Honey-Broiled Bananas, 138
- Mango & Dried Fruit Compote, 124
- Rosemary & Orange-Scented Apples, 128
- Winter Fruit Gratin, 130

G

Game hens
- Cranberry-Ginger Hens, 64
- Honey-Brushed Hens, 64

Garlic-Herb Sautéed Cherry Tomatoes, 107

Gazpacho, Garden-Fresh, with Mint, 23

Gelatin, Fresh Fruit, 132

Grains. *See Barley; Bulgur; Kasha; Quinoa; Rice*

Granola, Pumpkin Seed, 145

Grape & Raspberry-Poached Apples, 128

Grapefruit
- Citrus Salsa, 69

Greek-Style Chicken Salad, 62

Green Herb Broth, 25

Green & Orange Minestrone, 22

Green Rice & Peas, 114

Grilled New Potato Salad, 118

Grilled Pineapple with Maple Cream, 135

Grilled Vegetable Salad, 95

Guacamole, Spicy Pea , 18

H

Haddock, Vegetable-Topped Baked, 33

Ham
- Cilantro Rice with Ham & Corn, 114
- Orange-Mustard Ham Kebabs, 60

Honey-Broiled Bananas, 138

Honey-Brushed Hens, 64

Honey-Mustard Pork & Sweet Potatoes, 55

Honeydew, Roast Turkey Salad with, & Raspberries, 65

Hot Berry Sundaes, 123

I-J-K

Indian-Spiced Buttermilk, 108

Indian-Spiced Chick-Pea Pancake Mix, 140

Individual Pumpkin Soufflés, 126

Italian Bread Salad with Mozzarella & Roasted Peppers, 99

Italian Sausage Ragù with Fusilli, 77

Italian-Style Monkfish Stir-Fry, 32

Jamaican Jerked Chicken, 61

Kasha with Mushrooms, 113

Kiwifruit
- Banana-Kiwi Salsa, 69
- Winter Fruit Gratin, 130

L

Leeks, Tomato-Orange Braised, 100

Lemon-Curry Corn Chips, 17

Lemony Bulgur & Shrimp Salad, 49

Lemony Mushrooms, 110

Lettuce, Vegetarian Dutch, 112

Louisiana Rice & Bean Salad, 86

M

Mango & Dried Fruit Compote, 124

Maple Sweet Potatoes with Cranberries, 105

Marinara Sauce, Shiitake, 93

Meatless main courses
- Asian Noodle Salad, 83
- Bean & Butternut Chili, 96
- Brown Rice Pasta with Broccoli & Sun-Dried Tomatoes, 82
- Chick-Pea & Pesto Pizza, 89
- Cremini, Broccoli & Corn Salad, 98
- Fettuccine & Sugar Snaps with Almond-Orange Pesto, 88
- Grilled Vegetable Salad, 95
- Italian Bread Salad with Mozzarella & Roasted Peppers, 99
- Louisiana Rice & Bean Salad, 86
- Pasta with Asparagus & Snow Peas, 111
- Pasta with White Beans, Carrots & Tomatoes, 85
- Penne with Ratatouille Sauce, 90
- Polenta with Meatless Mushroom Sauce, 97
- Portobello Cheeseburgers, 94
- Potato-Asparagus Frittata, 141
- Rutabaga & Black Bean Couscous, 92
- Shiitake Marinara Sauce, 93
- Sloppy Josés, 81
- Spinach & Sesame Pasta Salad, 91
- Spinach, Tomato & Pasta Salad, 91
- Szechuan Stir-Fried Vegetables, 87
- Veggie Burgers, 84
- Winter Vegetable Couscous, 92

Mexican Pasta Salad Tonnato, 36

Mexican-Style Grilled Shrimp Cocktail, 16

Mexican-Style Turkey Burgers, 68

Minestrone, Green & Orange , 22

Monkfish Stir-Fry, Italian-Style, 32

Mousse, Berry Cheesecake, 131

Muffins
- Cinnamon-Apple Bran Muffins, 142
- Cinnamon-Pear Bran Muffins, 142

Mushrooms
- Chicken in Shiitake-Tomato Sauce, 76
- Cremini, Broccoli & Corn Salad, 98
- Curried Split Pea & Mushroom Soup, 28
- Kasha with Mushrooms, 113
- Lemony Mushrooms, 110
- Mushroom, Root Vegetable & Barley Soup, 27
- Polenta with Meatless Mushroom Sauce, 97
- Portobello Cheeseburgers, 94

Shiitake Marinara Sauce, 93

N-O

Niçoise Pita Pizza, 35
Oats
 Pear-Cranberry Crumble, 133
 Pumpkin Seed Granola, 145
 Toasted Oat Pancake Mix, 140
One-Crust Sour Cherry Pie, 136
Onions
 Chicken-Onion Soup, 63
 Onion Broth, 25
 Onion-Chicken Fajitas, 70
Orange-Currant Waffles, 139
Orange-Mustard Ham Kebabs, 60
Orange-Scented Zucchini Bread, 144
Oranges
 Citrus Salsa, 69
Oven-Steamed Bass with Thai-Style
 Vegetables, 31

P

Pancakes
 Chocolate Pancake Mix, 140
 Indian-Spiced Chick-Pea Pancake
 Mix, 140
 Toasted Oat Pancake Mix, 140
Parsnips
 Braised Pork & Root Vegetables, 52
 Mushroom, Root Vegetable & Barley
 Soup, 27
 Pot Roast with Winter Vegetables, 58
 Soy & Ginger Braised Beef, 52
 Winter Vegetable Couscous, 92
Pasta
 Asian Noodle Salad, 83
 Brown Rice Pasta with Broccoli &
 Sun-Dried Tomatoes, 82
 Capellini with Barbecued Pork &
 Vegetables, 57
 Chicken Curry with Wide Noodles, 66
 Fettuccine & Sugar Snaps with
 Almond-Orange Pesto, 88
 Italian Sausage Ragù with Fusilli, 77
 Mexican Pasta Salad Tonnato, 36
 Pasta Salad with Tonnato
 Sauce, 36
 Pasta with Asparagus & Snow Peas,
 111
 Pasta with Hunter-Style Chicken, 72

Pasta with Spicy Garlic-Shrimp Sauce,
 34
 Penne with Ratatouille Sauce, 90
 Potato Pasta with Tomatoes, Peppers
 & Cod, 39
 Rutabaga & Black Bean Couscous, 92
 Shiitake Marinara Sauce, 93
 Shrimp & Pasta Salad with Orange-
 Parsley Dressing, 42
 Spinach & Sesame Pasta Salad, 91
 Spinach, Tomato & Pasta Salad, 91
 Winter Vegetable Couscous, 92
Peaches
 Mango & Dried Fruit Compote, 124
Peanuts
 Quinoa with Peanuts & Dried
 Cherries, 117
Pears
 Pear-Cranberry Crumble, 133
 Pork Stew with Pears, 53
 Winter Fruit Gratin, 130
Peas. See also Chick-peas; Snow peas; Split
 peas; Sugar snap peas
 Bulgur with Asparagus & Peas, 115
 Green Rice & Peas, 114
 Spicy Pea Guacamole, 18
Penne with Ratatouille Sauce, 90
Peppers, bell
 Corn Pudding with Roasted Peppers &
 Scallions, 103
 Grilled Vegetable Salad, 95
 Italian Bread Salad with Mozzarella &
 Roasted Peppers, 99
 Roasted Pepper & Black Bean Soup, 24
 Unstuffed Peppers, 56
 Yellow Pepper & Chick-Pea Soup, 24
Peppery Pumpkin Risotto, 116
Pie, Sour Cherry, One-Crust, 136
Pineapple
 Breakfast Fruit Salad, 137
 Grilled Pineapple with Maple Cream,
 135
Pinto Beans, Baked, 104
Pizza
 Chick-Pea & Pesto Pizza, 89
 Niçoise Pita Pizza, 35
Plums, dried (prunes)
 Mango & Dried Fruit Compote, 124
Polenta with Meatless Mushroom Sauce,
 97

Pork
 Apple-Glazed Pork Tenderloin, 59
 Braised Pork & Root Vegetables, 52
 Capellini with Barbecued Pork &
 Vegetables, 57
 Currant-Glazed Pork Tenderloin, 59
 Honey-Mustard Pork & Sweet
 Potatoes, 55
 Pork Stew with Pears, 53
Portobello Cheeseburgers, 94
Pot Roast with Winter Vegetables, 58
Potato Pasta with Tomatoes, Peppers &
 Cod, 39
Potato-Asparagus Frittata, 141
Potatoes
 Grilled New Potato Salad, 118
 Pot Roast with Winter Vegetables, 58
 Potato-Asparagus Frittata, 141
 Vegetarian Dutch Lettuce, 112
Provençal Chicken Stew, 71
Prunes. See Plums, dried
Pudding, Pumpkin Cheesecake, 134
Pumpkin
 Individual Pumpkin Soufflés, 126
 Peppery Pumpkin Risotto, 116
 Pumpkin Cheesecake Puddings, 134
 Spiced Caribbean Pumpkin Soup, 19
Pumpkin Seed Granola, 145

Q-R

Quinoa with Peanuts & Dried Cherries,
 117
Raspberries
 Hot Berry Sundaes, 123
 Roast Turkey Salad with Honeydew &
 Raspberries, 65
Red Bean, Rice & Shrimp Salad, 86
Red snapper. See Snapper
Rice
 Cilantro Rice with Ham & Corn, 114
 Creamy Carrot & Rice Soup, 20
 Green Rice & Peas, 114
 Louisiana Rice & Bean Salad, 86
 Peppery Pumpkin Risotto, 116
 Red Bean, Rice & Shrimp Salad, 86
 Rice-Stuffed Butternut Squash, 101
Roast Turkey Breast with Garlic, Lemon
 & Basil, 80
Roast Turkey Salad with Honeydew &
 Raspberries, 65

Recipes for Weight Loss

Roasted Pepper & Black Bean Soup, 24
Rosemary & Orange-Scented Apples, 128
Rutabaga & Black Bean Couscous, 92

S

Salad dressing
    Carrot-Orange Dressing, 119
    Fat-Free Balsamic Vinaigrette, 119
    Fat-Free Pineapple-Tarragon Dressing, 119
Salads, main-course
    Asian Barbecued Chicken Salad, 67
    Asian Noodle Salad, 83
    Barbecued Chicken Salad, 67
    Cremini, Broccoli & Corn Salad, 98
    Greek-Style Chicken Salad, 62
    Grilled Vegetable Salad, 95
    Italian Bread Salad with Mozzarella & Roasted Peppers, 99
    Lemony Bulgur & Shrimp Salad, 49
    Louisiana Rice & Bean Salad, 86
    Mexican Pasta Salad Tonnato, 36
    Pasta Salad with Tonnato Sauce, 36
    Red Bean, Rice & Shrimp Salad, 86
    Roast Turkey Salad with Honeydew & Raspberries, 65
    Shrimp & Barley Salad with Lemon-Cilantro Dressing, 42
    Shrimp & Pasta Salad with Orange-Parsley Dressing, 42
    Spinach & Sesame Pasta Salad, 91
    Spinach, Tomato & Pasta Salad, 91
    Tomato-Bean Salad with Orzo, 121
    Turkey & Sweet Potato Salad with Honey-Mustard Dressing, 75
Salads, side-dish
    Breakfast Fruit Salad, 137
    Cabbage & Apple Slaw, 120
    Coleslaw, 120
    Grilled New Potato Salad, 118
    Tomato & Cannellini Salad with Roasted Garlic Dressing, 121
    Vegetable Slaw with Lemon-Mustard Dressing, 122
    Vegetarian Dutch Lettuce, 112
Salsa
    Banana-Kiwi Salsa, 69
    Citrus Salsa, 69
    Corn Salsa, 69

Sandwiches. *See also Burgers*
    Sloppy Josés, 81
Sausage, turkey
    Italian Sausage Ragù with Fusilli, 77
Sautéed Scallops Niçoise, 48
Sautéed Shrimp with Garlic & Spinach, 46
Scallops
    Sautéed Scallops Niçoise, 48
    Scallops with Sautéed Tomatoes, 107
Sesame Asparagus & Snow Peas, 111
Shakes
    Carrot, Apple & Ginger Shake, 108
    Indian-Spiced Buttermilk, 108
    Yogurt-Cucumber Shake, 108
Shellfish. *See specific types*
Shiitake mushrooms
    Chicken in Shiitake-Tomato Sauce, 76
    Curried Split Pea & Mushroom Soup , 28
    Oven-Steamed Bass with Thai-Style Vegetables, 31
    Pasta with Hunter-Style Chicken, 72
    Polenta with Meatless Mushroom Sauce, 97
    Shiitake Marinara Sauce, 93
    Vegetarian Dutch Lettuce, 112
Shrimp
    Lemony Bulgur & Shrimp Salad, 49
    Mexican-Style Grilled Shrimp Cocktail, 16
    Pasta with Spicy Garlic-Shrimp Sauce, 34
    Red Bean, Rice & Shrimp Salad, 86
    Sautéed Shrimp with Garlic & Spinach, 46
    Shrimp & Barley Salad with Lemon-Cilantro Dressing, 42
    Shrimp & Pasta Salad with Orange-Parsley Dressing, 42
    Shrimp & Sweet Potato Curry, 38
    Spicy Shrimp Chowder, 51
    Tomato-Shrimp Bisque, 30
Slaw
    Cabbage & Apple Slaw, 120
    Coleslaw, 120
    Vegetable Slaw with Lemon-Mustard Dressing, 122
Sloppy Josés, 81

Snapper
    Chili-Broiled Snapper, 50
    Curry-Broiled Snapper, 50
Snow peas
    Pasta with Asparagus & Snow Peas, 111
    Sesame Asparagus & Snow Peas, 111
    Szechuan Stir-Fried Vegetables, 87
Sole. *See also Flounder*
    Spinach-Stuffed Sole, 41
Soufflés, Individual Pumpkin, 126
Soups. *See also Broths*
    Apple-Winter Squash Soup, 26
    Carrot & Barley Soup with Basil, 20
    Chicken-Onion Soup, 63
    Creamy Carrot & Rice Soup, 20
    Curried Split Pea & Mushroom Soup, 28
    Garden-Fresh Gazpacho with Mint, 23
    Green & Orange Minestrone, 22
    Mushroom, Root Vegetable & Barley Soup, 27
    Roasted Pepper & Black Bean Soup, 24
    Spiced Caribbean Pumpkin Soup, 19
    Spicy Clam Chowder, 51
    Spicy Shrimp Chowder, 51
    Spinach & Lemon Soup, 29
    Tomato-Shrimp Bisque, 30
    Tomato-Vegetable Chowder, 21
    Yellow Pepper & Chick-Pea Soup, 24
Soy cheese
    Italian Bread Salad with Mozzarella & Roasted Peppers, 99
Soy & Ginger Braised Beef, 52
Soy protein. *See also TVP*
    Chocolate Pancake Mix, 140
    Orange-Currant Waffles, 139
    Toasted Oat Pancake Mix, 140
Spiced Caribbean Pumpkin Soup, 19
Spicy Clam Chowder, 51
Spicy Pea Guacamole, 18
Spicy Shrimp Chowder, 51
Spinach
    Green & Orange Minestrone, 22
    Sautéed Shrimp with Garlic & Spinach, 46
    Spinach & Lemon Soup, 29
    Spinach & Sesame Pasta Salad, 91
    Spinach, Tomato & Pasta Salad, 91
    Spinach with Garlic & Raisins, 102

Spinach-Stuffed Sole, 41
Split Pea & Mushroom Soup, Curried, 28
Squash, summer
    Orange-Scented Zucchini Bread, 144
    Penne with Ratatouille Sauce, 90
    Vegetable Slaw with Lemon-Mustard
        Dressing, 122
Squash, winter
    Apple-Winter Squash Soup, 26
    Baked Butternut Squash, 101
    Bean & Butternut Chili, 96
    Rice-Stuffed Butternut Squash, 101
Stews
    Bean & Butternut Chili, 96
    Fish Stew Arrabbiata, 45
    Pork Stew with Pears, 53
    Provençal Chicken Stew, 71
    Shrimp & Sweet Potato Curry, 38
Strawberries
    Fresh Fruit Gelatin, 132
    Strawberry Long Cake, 125
Striped Bass Provençale, 44
Sugar snap peas
    Fettuccine & Sugar Snaps with
        Almond-Orange Pesto, 88
    Sugar Snap Peas with Basil &
        Tomatoes, 109
Sundaes, Hot Berry, 123
Sweet potatoes
    Feta-Topped Baked Chicken &
        Vegetables, 62
    Honey-Mustard Pork & Sweet
        Potatoes, 55
    Maple Sweet Potatoes with
        Cranberries, 105
    Mushroom, Root Vegetable & Barley
        Soup, 27
    Pot Roast with Winter Vegetables, 58
    Turkey & Sweet Potato Salad with
        Honey-Mustard Dressing, 75
Shrimp & Sweet Potato Curry, 38
Sweet & Sour Red Cabbage, 106
Sweet & Sour Turkey Stir-Fry, 73
Swordfish Milanese, 43
Szechuan Stir-Fried Vegetables, 87

T

Thai Tuna Burger, 47
Toasted Oat Pancake Mix, 140

Tofu
    Grilled Vegetable Salad, 95
    Szechuan Stir-Fried Vegetables, 87
    Veggie Burgers, 84
Tomatoes
    Chicken, Broccoli & Tomato Stir-Fry,
        78
    Chicken in Shiitake-Tomato Sauce, 76
    Feta-Topped Baked Chicken &
        Vegetables, 62
    Garden-Fresh Gazpacho with
        Mint, 23
    Garlic-Herb Sautéed Cherry
        Tomatoes, 107
    Pasta with Hunter-Style Chicken, 72
    Pasta with White Beans, Carrots &
        Tomatoes, 85
    Penne with Ratatouille Sauce, 90
    Scallops with Sautéed Tomatoes, 107
    Shiitake Marinara Sauce, 93
    Sloppy Josés, 81
    Sugar Snap Peas with Basil &
        Tomatoes, 109
    Tomato & Cannellini Salad with
        Roasted Garlic Dressing, 121
    Tomato-Bean Salad with Orzo, 121
    Tomato-Orange Braised Leeks, 100
    Tomato-Shrimp Bisque, 30
    Tomato-Vegetable Chowder, 21
Tortillas. See also Fajitas
    Chili-Lime Corn Chips, 17
    Lemon-Curry Corn Chips, 17
Tuna
    Dilled Tuna Burger, 47
    Mexican Pasta Salad Tonnato, 36
    Niçoise Pita Pizza, 35
    Pasta Salad with Tonnato Sauce, 36
    Thai Tuna Burger, 47
Turkey
    Mexican-Style Turkey Burgers, 68
    Roast Turkey Breast with Garlic,
        Lemon & Basil, 80
    Roast Turkey Salad with Honeydew &
        Raspberries, 65
    Sweet & Sour Turkey Stir-Fry, 73
    Turkey & Sweet Potato Salad with
        Honey-Mustard Dressing, 75
Turnips
    Soy & Ginger Braised Beef, 52

TVP
    Polenta with Meatless Mushroom
        Sauce, 97
    Sloppy Josés, 81

U-V

Unstuffed Peppers, 56
Vegetable side dishes. See also specific types
    Baked Butternut Squash, 101
    Chili Corn Pudding, 103
    Corn Pudding with Roasted Peppers &
        Scallions, 103
    Garlic-Herb Sautéed Cherry
        Tomatoes, 107
    Lemony Mushrooms, 110
    Maple Sweet Potatoes with
        Cranberries, 105
    Rice-Stuffed Butternut Squash, 101
    Sesame Asparagus & Snow Peas, 111
    Spinach with Garlic & Raisins, 102
    Sugar Snap Peas with Basil &
        Tomatoes, 109
    Sweet & Sour Red Cabbage, 106
    Tomato-Orange Braised Leeks, 100
Vegetable Slaw with Lemon-Mustard
    Dressing, 122
Vegetable-Topped Baked Haddock, 33
Vegetarian Dutch Lettuce, 112
Veggie Burgers, 84
Vinaigrette. See Salad dressing

W-Y-Z

Waffles, Orange-Currant , 139
Winter Fruit Gratin, 130
Winter Squash. See Squash, winter
Winter Vegetable Couscous, 92
Yellow Pepper & Chick-Pea Soup, 24
Yogurt-Cucumber Shake, 108
Zucchini
    Orange-Scented Zucchini Bread, 144
    Penne with Ratatouille Sauce, 90
    Vegetable Slaw with Lemon-Mustard
        Dressing, 122

LAWRENCE J. CHESKIN, M.D., graduated from Dartmouth Medical School and completed a fellowship in gastroenterology at Yale-New Haven Hospital in Connecticut. Currently, he is an associate professor of international health and human nutrition at the Johns Hopkins Bloomberg School of Public Health and an associate professor of medicine at the Johns Hopkins School of Medicine. Dr. Cheskin is also the director of the Johns Hopkins Weight Management Center.

In his research, Dr. Cheskin has studied the effects of medications on body weight, gastrointestinal effects of olestra, how cigarette smoking relates to dieting and body weight, and the effectiveness of lifestyle changes in weight loss and weight maintenance. He is also the author of three books: *Losing Weight for Good, New Hope for People with Weight Problems*, and *Better Homes and Gardens 3 Steps to Weight Loss*. Dr. Cheskin has appeared on television news programs and delivered lectures to both professional and lay audiences on the topics of weight loss and weight management.

LORA BROWN WILDER, Sc.D., M.S., R.D., a registered dietitian, received her M.S. in nutrition from the University of Maryland and her Sc.D. in public health from Johns Hopkins University. She is currently an assistant professor at the Johns Hopkins School of Medicine, and is also affiliated with the USDA and the University of Maryland's Department of Nutrition and Food Science. Dr. Wilder has served on various advisory committees related to nutrition, including the American Heart Association and the National Institutes of Health, and helped set up the first Johns Hopkins Preventive Cardiology Program.

In her research, Dr. Wilder has studied the effects of coffee on fatty acids and investigated behavioral strategies to reduce coronary risk factors. Her current research is in the area of dietary assessment methodology. She contributed to *Nutritional Management: The Johns Hopkins Handbook* and has been published in such journals as *Circulation, American Journal of Medicine*, and *Journal of the American Medical Association*.

SIMEON MARGOLIS, M.D., Ph.D., a professor of medicine and biological chemistry at the Johns Hopkins University School of Medicine, is the medical editor for *The Johns Hopkins Medical Letter: Health After 50* and the consulting medical editor for *The Johns Hopkins Cookbook Library*.

The Johns Hopkins Cookbook Library is published by Medletter Associates, Inc.

Rodney Friedman	Publisher
Kate Slate	Executive Editor
Sandra Rose Gluck	Test Kitchen Director, Food Editor
Timothy Jeffs	Art Director
Maureen Mulhern-White	Senior Writer
Patricia Kaupas	Writer/Researcher
James W. Brown	Associate Editor